DOUBLE-DUTY DECORATING

DOUBLE-DUTY DECORATING

VIRGINIA CARRY

Illustrated by Robert Penny

Charles Scribner's Sons   New York

Text copyright © 1983 by Virginia Carry
Illustrations copyright © Charles Scribner's Sons

Library of Congress Cataloging in Publication Data

Carry, Virginia.
  Double-duty decorating.

  Includes index.
  1. Interior decoration—Handbooks, manuals, etc.
I. Title.
NK2115.C32 1983   747.213   83-11616
ISBN 0-684-17949-0

1 3 5 7 9 11 13 15 17 19   F/C   20 18 16 14 12 10 8 6 4 2

Printed in the United States of America.

To Peter

ACKNOWLEDGMENTS

First, I would like to thank illustrator Robert Penny for the enthusiasm he showed for this project, the many many ideas he contributed, and his patience—"Where did you say you wanted that lamp?"—of which he had a seemingly inexhaustible supply.

Thanks so much to all the people who allowed me into their homes so their double-duty rooms could appear in this book: Tom and Corine Fitzpatrick, Tom and Harriet Burnette, Dick and Christine Roth, Jeffrey and Hanna Moskin, Sarah Pileggi, and Bettan Pritchard. I am grateful for the time that designers Jeffrey Weiss, Susan Zises Green, Robert Hart, Scott Kemper, Robert Lone, and Jean Weiner and Paul Schaefer took from their busy schedules to spend with me.

I want to especially thank Margot Gunther and Christine Roth, from whom I have learned so much about my subject. Thanks also to Halo Lighting and Yorktowne, Inc., for the ideas they contributed, to John Hummer for lending me office space when I needed it, to Grace Bowen, who kept my house running without a hitch, and to Megan Schembre, who spent so much time unscrambling the manuscript.

Finally I would like to express my warmest thanks and gratitude to Maron Waxman, who suggested this book and cajoled me into finishing it, and to my husband, Peter, whose love and advice are always there when I need them.

Virginia Carry

CONTENTS

Introduction   xi
 1. The Right Combination   1
 2. Dividing Lines   5
 3. Living Rooms with More   18
 4. Double-Duty Dining Rooms   32
 5. Better Bedrooms   40
 6. Combination Kitchens   50
 7. Stashing the Kids   63
 8. Working at Home   75
 9. The Guesting Game   87
10. Nooks and Crannies   95
11. Shelf Life   112
12. Lofty Ideas   123
13. Resisting the Apartment Squeeze   130
14. Studio Strategies   139
15. Designing for the Double Life   150
Designers   165
Resource List   167
Index   173

INTRODUCTION

A few years ago, just as I was wishing our apartment would grow another room, we grew another person instead. With one-room cabins selling for six figures in our neighborhood, we found we would have to make do with the home we had, although the home we had was smaller than the home we might have liked. It was then that I became a double-duty decorator.

That's what this book is about: how to make your house seem bigger than it really is. When your house suddenly has to accommodate another child or a new career, the trick is to turn one room into two—one living area with two or more distinct functions, none of which interferes with the others. In other words, double-duty decorating. This is not to suggest combining a bedroom with a roller disco. It isn't a bad idea, however, to toss out a lot of outdated conventions. The notion that dining rooms are just for dining is prehistoric. If the only times you actually eat in it are Thanksgiving and Christmas, then this room is a monument to a way of life that isn't yours and is an unfortunate waste of space. How much living goes on in your living room? Is the real heart of the house the kitchen or the family room? Think about it.

After you have thought about it awhile, you'll have a firm idea of which areas of your house get too much use, which too little. With a bit of constructive juggling, those dead spots can be injected with life and can ease the crunch in the busier areas, thus making your house or apartment more livable and utilitarian than you ever thought possible. As needs change— and for most families they do every eight to ten years—you can reshuffle the deck. Your residence should suit the times of your life—and the best part about approaching these changes through decorating is that it allows a lot of variation without making expensive structural changes.

When our apartment had to make room for child number two, we found we could still have a den—previously situated in a bedroom—if we put it into the kitchen. The rest followed easily. The old den reverted to a bedroom; the washer and dryer, formerly in the kitchen, moved into a closet; the dining room was partitioned to absorb my office, which had also been in the kitchen, and my husband's desk found a home in the foyer, which had previously served no useful function at all. As a result of this game of musical rooms, there's not an inch of wasted space in our apartment, and it's a better place to live in than it was before.

As you consider reallocating the space in your house, remember there are plenty of terrific combinations to ponder. Two of the better ones are joining the kitchen with the dining room or the family room. But this is just a beginning. Rooms can be divided into day and night functions: office by day, bedroom at night. Living rooms can double as short-term guest rooms. Hobby areas can be built into dining rooms or dens. Some spaces are sacred. In our house we have a "grown-ups only" living room, used mostly for entertaining and reading the Sunday papers. We just couldn't bear to give it up—and we didn't. But because changes in decor aren't forever, we could have chosen to use the living room as a family room for now and changed it back to an adult retreat later. That's one of the beauties of double-duty decorating. Another advantage is that while you seem to have more space, your utility bill may not increase at all.

This book will help you in your double-duty decision making. And sometimes a fresh eye, either that of a friend or a professional, can spot the right approach when you feel blinded by the complexity of it all. But once you get the right ideas, you'll discover that two-in-one decorating is not only a pleasure but, for many families today, the only way to live.

DOUBLE-DUTY
DECORATING

1 THE RIGHT COMBINATION

Looking for a new house today isn't fun. In fact, it's considerably less fun than going to the dentist or getting a parking ticket. That's one reason Americans have become less mobile than they've been at any time since World War II. Houses and co-op or condominium apartments cost more than ever, and mortgage dollars seem even scarcer than places to live. The situation affects everyone who owns a residence or who would like to. Thus, homeowners today are finding that they can't afford the larger houses they want and must continue living in homes they may have outgrown despite new babies, new children as a result of remarriage, or a change of career.

CREATING MORE SPACE

When you decide to write the great American novel, go into the real estate business, design clothes, open a typing service, or become a public relations consultant, your home will be your base of operations, at least initially.

Naturally, your thoughts may turn to remodeling. Making major structural changes, however, can cost as much today as an entire house did fifteen years ago. Apartment dwellers may be limited by what the landlord or the condo/co-op board will allow, and few things that are ripped out now can be replaced at anything near their original cost.

One approach to creating more space is to do a little remodeling and considerably more redecorating. Decorating is a bargain when you weigh the costs of paint and fabric against those of plumbing or electrical work.

The best way to begin is to make a list of everything you want to have space for.

It might look like this:	The resolution might be this:
Office for daytime work Family room because living room is always a wreck Eat-in kitchen	Modify bedroom to double as office Turn one end of living room into formal dining area (new combination living/dining room will revert to adult pursuits) Knock down wall between dining room and kitchen to make family room with eating bar.

TAKE A NEW LOOK AT OLD ROOMS

To find the double-duty potential in your home, you'll need to evaluate each room and decide whether you use it too much or too little. Are there rooms that are too big for what goes on in them and others that are so small they are hopelessly cramped? Some very large rooms suffer from dead spots—for example, a living room where no one ever sits in certain chairs because they're out in left field. By concentrating the conversation group in one end of the room, you open up the other end to more useful possibilities, such as music playing or listening, an office, or a dining area.

Begin your search for wasted space at the front door. A foyer should be an attractive welcomer, but if space is at a premium you can't afford to waste any. Maybe your entry hall could hold a piano—if not a grand at least an upright—or a desk, or an armoire for extra storage. Next, scrutinize your dining room, frequently the least busy room in the house. It's rarely used for more than one meal a day, and in some houses it's called into service a lot less than that. Dining rooms can be combined with kitchens, usually to the advantage of both, or they can become part-time offices, or playrooms, or any number of other things. Even closets can contribute to spacious living when they are transformed into something more than mere storage facilities. Upstairs landings, sun porches, and the occasional odd bathroom can all be recycled into active living areas. An extra bathroom can be an ideal photographer's darkroom.

Sometimes removing a wall will produce the desired effect, and it's certainly cheaper than building one. Combining a tiny kitchen with the small dining room next to it will result in a much more attractive space that you'll enjoy being in, partly because you'll actually have room to walk around. Two cramped, adjoining bedrooms—the kind in which you've got to move the bed to open a bureau drawer—might work far better as one larger room where space has been allotted for sewing, working, and guest accommodations.

PEACEFUL COEXISTENCE

When you're sizing up a room for double duty, part of the job is figuring out what functions you can put together successfully. If you do serious work at home, an office in the kitchen isn't a good idea because there will be too much noise and traffic while you're trying to concentrate. However, doing household accounts in the kitchen does make sense, and usually it's not difficult to find a spot for a small office there. If you share a bedroom, don't plan on having your hobby area there too if you work on it at night. You'd be disturbing whoever shares the room with you. Keep the TV out of rooms where you want to read or think. Try to combine day and night activities in the same room instead of day and day and night and night, unless the two pastimes are totally compatible.

There are a few natural go-togethers: the bedroom/office, the living room/dining room, the kitchen/family room, the den/guest room. Sometimes just adding the appropriate piece of furniture—desk, sleep sofa, dining table, or whatever—to what's already in a room, and arranging the furniture in a new way, will create the dual-purpose room you need. Other situations call for work spaces that disappear behind curtains, shades, or screens, so that the double-duty aspect of a room isn't obvious to visitors.

Look at your home and at your way of doing things for decorating cues. If your sewing, hobby, or work area is likely to be creatively cluttered, it should probably be located in a space that can be hidden from view so you won't waste time cleaning it up or feeling guilty if you don't.

The amount of space you need or want to devote to an activity is also a consideration. How much room do you really need to have for your stamp collection? Perhaps it could be stored conveniently and attractively in a section of a wall unit with shelves for stamp books and a fold-down desk for working on them. Is working at home something you do full time or only on an occasional basis? You can tuck a family office in any number of spots, but files, drafting tables, and the like are more difficult to find places for.

PRACTICAL TACTICS

Naturally there are some pitfalls to double-duty decorating. It's disheartening to discover that while the drawers under the campaign bed in your new combination den/guest room are wonderfully roomy, you can't get into them without moving two chairs and a table. If using the dining room of your office/dining room requires that you shift a ton of furniture and fixtures, you won't use it once a month, let alone once a day. The best double-duty decorating solutions require a minimum amount of moving and shaking to transform one of the room's functions into the other. While not everything can be effortless, the switches should take only a few minutes, and you should be able to make them alone.

Movable furniture should be movable! It should be on casters, if possible, or be lightweight enough that you can shift it around without slipping a disk. It's fine to make up the divan for an occasional overnight guest, but sleeping on it every night would be a big pain in the neck, not to mention the back. If you have a convertible sofa that's going to be used frequently, choose one that the bedding can stay on. It's enough trouble to take the cushions off and fold out a piece of convertible furniture without adding the extra work of making it up every time. Any surface that's going to double as something else—a desk/dining table, for instance—should have a catchall nearby so that you can sweep the task in progress into it and the table can get on to its next job.

All of this is much easier if tidiness is your way of life. In homes without attics or basements and in apartments with limited closet space, there's just no room for a lifetime collection of get-well cards or all your sartorial errors. Any decorator will tell you that it's impossible to create attractive and functional surroundings if the people who live in them don't make some effort to have a place for everything and everything in its place. That goes double for double-duty rooms.

Yet shuffling your home around can be gratifying. It'll feel like new again, even though it's not. You'll also be saving the cost of moving, and you won't be trading up to a larger house that would be much more expensive to heat and light. Perhaps most important, you'll have learned to look at this house, and any future ones, as pure space to organize in the way that suits you and your way of life best.

2 DIVIDING LINES

Can you have your cake and eat it too? This is the question the multifunctional room asks. To divide and unify at the same time, you need a few basic decorative devices at your finger tips. The most important one is the room divider. The ideas suggested in this chapter can be adapted to give a subtle or not-so-subtle sense of division and, while the essential ingredients vary, the principles remain the same whether you're dividing a living room, a kitchen, or a bedroom.

For example, how do you subdivide a large room into centers of various activities but still keep it visually unified? After all, one of the assets of a big room is its bigness. It's a shame to chop up a great flowing space into eye- and psyche-jarring cubicles. In the best of all possible worlds, a room would retain its airiness while unobtrusively doing many jobs.

Everyone wants to preserve the spacious look of a spacious room, but some kind of dividing line is often desirable to indicate where one of the room's functions ends and another begins. Too bad you can't just paint a dotted line on the floor! But before you invest in something that wouldn't be a bad substitute for the Great Wall, consider the following:

- Does the divider need to be a separate entity, or can the feeling of division be achieved with an artful arrangement of furniture or floor or wall treatments?

- If a real divider is called for, must it be opaque enough to hide some eyesore—a storage area or a cluttered home office—or do you want to see the rest of the room through it?

You may need only a single panel to screen off a corner or to create an entry-way when the front door opens directly into the living room. Pictured here is a length of old lace, sandwiched between pieces of Lucite and hung from screw eyes mounted in the ceiling. It's secured to the floor in the same manner. A stained-glass panel would be equally effective.

• Is the divider to remain stationary or must it move back and forth as the room goes from working to sleeping, or from living to dining, or to and from another combination of uses?

ROOMS WITHIN ROOMS

Short of building a permanent wall, there are a number of ways to go about subdividing a room. Sometimes merely rearranging the furniture will do the trick—and you can't beat the price. This technique involves creating natural dividing lines by facing some pieces of furniture toward each other and others away from each other. For example, two sofas arranged at right angles can create an instant room-within-a-room by making a natural division between this seating area and a dining table and chairs that can be placed behind one of the sofas. Right and left chaise longues or a pair of sofas facing each other across a fireplace or in front of a distinguished piece of furniture that is the room's focal point—an antique armoire or a beautiful Oriental cabinet—also provide a self-contained conversation area. Whatever isn't in that area is distinctly separate from that part of the room.

Space-saving arrangements like these are a good reason to check out the back of every piece of furniture before you buy it. Workmanship on the back of upholstered pieces should be just as painstaking as it is on the front. It's a good idea to make sure the pieces are attractive to look at from all angles. When buying bookcases, chests, and occasional pieces, look for those with finished backs, so that even if you put them up against the wall to begin with, you have the freedom to move them around later.

PLATFORMS

A change of floor level makes a room more interesting to look at and is an emphatic demarcation line. Although very few homes have a sunken living room, it is possible to create the reverse by building a platform to step up to at one end of a room or even in the center, like an island. And don't confine this to just the living room; platforms work well in bedrooms and family rooms, too. Most platforms can be constructed of two by fours and plywood panels. The total weight can usually be borne by most floors, but it would be wise to check before you begin. Some platforms have hinged or removable top sections so that you can use the space inside for storage, an excellent feature that adds very little to the cost of construction. The surface of the platform can be used for the placement of chairs and sofas, for a dining ensemble in a combination living room/dining room, for sleeping quarters in a bedroom/office, or for anything else you want. If the platform is a large one, you may even subdivide it by a deft furniture arrangement or a low screen and end up with three distinct areas instead of two.

Interior designers often do far more elaborate things with platforms

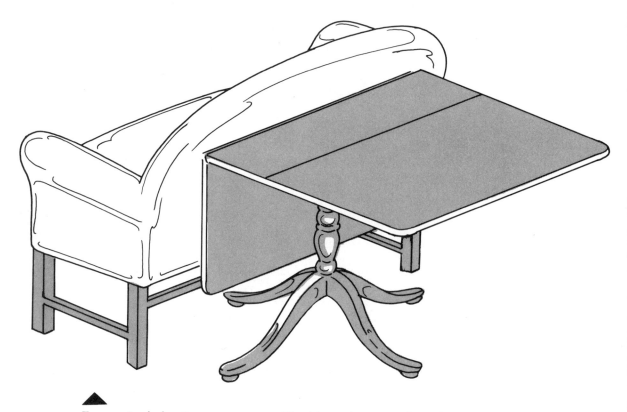

Even a simple furniture arrangement like this works to set off one half of a room from another. A drop-leaf table positioned behind a small sofa breaks a room into conversation and dining or working areas. You can pull the table out all the way for dining or fold both leaves down and use it as a sofa table with plants or a small collection of objects or photographs.

than the simple one or two steps up at one end of a room that we are talking about here. One idea you can copy from them is to round the corners of the structure—you will probably need a professional carpenter to do this—and then carpet the platform. The result will be a more elegant look.

Carpet, by the way, is probably the best covering for a platform because it not only hides any construction flaws but also is comfortable to sit on, particularly if a layer of padding is installed underneath.

LIGHTING

Lighting can be an effective divider, but obviously the results are going to be most apparent at night. This method makes use of such fixtures as track lights and/or individual spots, wall washers, and downlights. All of these spotlight specific areas of a room instead of casting their glow indiscriminately over a wide area the way traditional lamps do. If the living and dining areas of a room have individual lighting spheres, the table and its dirty dishes will "disappear" when the lights are extinguished. Track lights focused on a seating area in the center of a room make it stand out like a stage. The same idea works for an island bed, but for more intimacy and less glare, the lamps should be adjustable ceiling-hung models or table-top spots equipped with dimmers. This lighting style works best if you borrow a trick from theatrical designers—paint both the ceiling and the lighting fixtures installed on them in the same dark tone. A dark color obscures where the fixture ends and the ceiling begins.

ON THE FLOOR

Don't forget the floor when you're trying to plan your great divide. An area rug is one of the easiest ways to separate area A from area B. While it's not necessary for all the furniture to fit inside the rectangle the rug describes, at least half of the pieces should have all of their feet on it. Area rugs look great on bare floors as well as on top of wall-to-wall carpeting, an especially good idea if you have inherited a house or apartment already carpeted with something you don't like. But if you're ordering for the first time, wall-to-wall carpeting can be designed with a block of contrasting color or with contrasting bands that can be used as borders to outline smaller areas within the larger one.

Painting the floor is yet another way to suggest a division. Floors can be completely painted, with contrasting colors highlighting smaller interior areas in much the same way that area rugs do when laid on top of wall-to-wall carpeting. If you hesitate at the thought of covering up the wood grain, both natural-finish and painted floors are perfect candidates for stenciling. Stenciling is a charming way to mark off one area from another

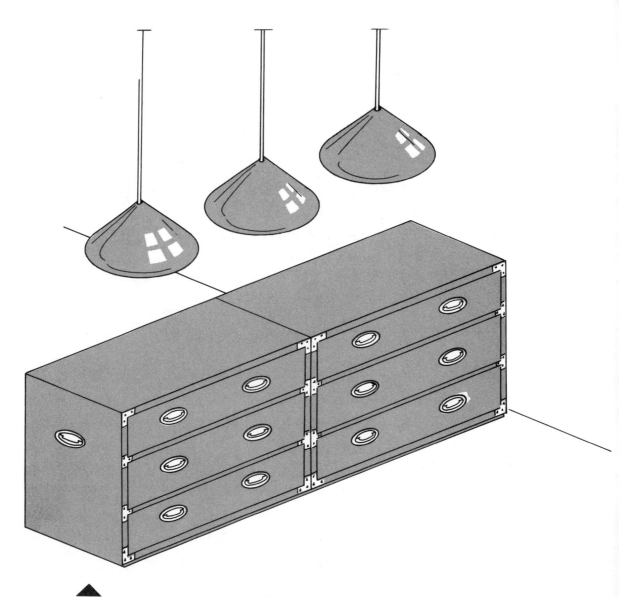

A couple of low chests or a set of low bookcases placed at right angles to a wall or free standing in the center of a room are a much more impressive divider when given emphasis by a row of hanging lamps. The drawers could open into your dining area to provide storage space for linen and silver, thus doubling as a buffet. The chests also could be part of a home office setup. You might want to face the drawer units in opposite directions. A somewhat airier look could be achieved by substituting a Parsons table for the chests, but then you would lose your storage space.

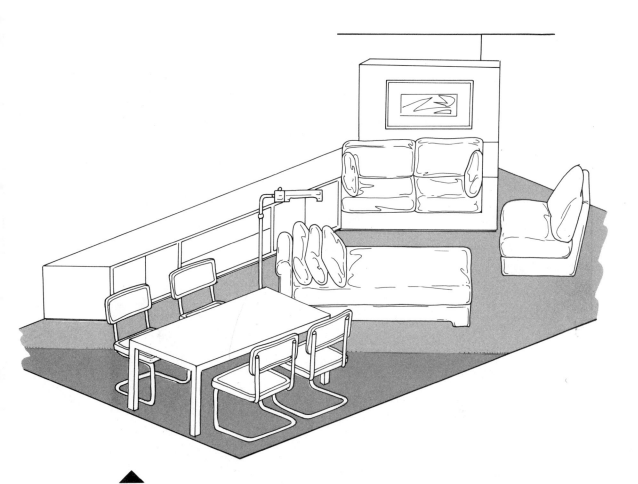

Here's a room designed on the diagonal in which the wall-to-wall carpeting helps to distinguish one area from another. The edges of the darker and lighter carpeting describe a neat line between the living and the dining areas of this small room. While doing things on the diagonal helps relieve the boxiness of small rooms, it's a rather modern treatment. A contrasting rectangle set into the background color of the rug creates a more traditional look and indicates a seating area just as effectively. A bar is concealed behind the built-in sofa unit in the corner of the room.

There's nothing tricky here, just a combination living room/dining room divided by a latticework screen. In a room like this one, you're not trying to erect the Berlin Wall. All you want to do is give both areas more intimacy than a simple furniture arrangement could. A wicker screen divides but doesn't completely block air or hints of a charming view. Any screen must be sturdy enough so that it's not in danger of falling over at a touch. You may anchor your screen to the floor with angle irons if it's a bit too shaky for comfort.

When the kitchen directly adjoins a living space, the way a pullman kitchen does, it's nice to be able to hide the food preparation area. A solid three-panel screen anchored to the floor with angle irons is an attractive alternative to disguising the kitchen with blinds or folding doors. The one pictured here has panels of shirred fabric on one side while the inside frame—with the use of a center support rib as a shelf and the installation of screw hooks—has been turned into auxiliary storage space for spices and cookware, as well as a nook for a handy butcher block. You could, of course, use flat panels of fabric to cover the screen and line an inside panel with a pegboard to hang up your kitchen gadget collection.

without painting wide expanses of floor. A multitude of stencil patterns is available in colonial as well as contemporary motifs.

WORKING WITH WALLS

Doing something different with walls also helps give the illusion of a division. Wall graphics are dramatic and can be designed to foster the feeling of two-rooms-in-one—particularly if the graphics are put on the ceiling as well as the walls. Almost anyone can paint a graphic with the help of a few rolls of masking tape to keep the edges even. Just don't take the tape off until the paint is dry. Wallpapering one end of a room and painting the other end in a coordinate shade is another easy way to let your room take sides. Many wallpaper lines now have matching borders which you purchase by the yard. You might continue this trim around the windows and doorways, under the crown molding, or above the baseboard in the painted area to unify the room a bit more.

Mirroring several feet of a long side wall, top to bottom, is a very effective way to divide a long, narrow room into two sectors, and it makes it seem wider at the same time. Adding wood moldings, which are conspicuously missing from newer buildings, to create panels for wallpaper or merely to give a lift to otherwise uninteresting walls may also give you the divided feeling you're looking for. Simply put the moldings on one part of the wall and not the other, or vary the wallpaper within the molding.

STANDING DIVIDERS

If moving the furniture around isn't enough and you're not satisfied with the above visual tricks, the next step is to install some kind of real room divider. Among the cheapest and most versatile is the folding screen. Filigree screens allow you a glimpse of what is behind them and let some air through. A translucent Japanese rice paper screen glows pleasantly when it's backlighted, while a lacquered Chinese screen presents an opaque barrier to the eye. In fact, you can find ready-made screens in every style imaginable, or you can hinge them together yourself—preferably with piano hinges so the panels can bend both ways. You can make a screen from all manner of materials: doors, shutters, or pieces of plywood, or you can construct one from a succession of open wood frames and fill in the panels with shirred fabric to match your decor. Solid panels can be covered with hand-painted murals, decoupage, wallpaper, or decorative moldings. It's your move.

Some dividers are ceiling hung from tracks, with flat panels that slide back and forth or open and close in much the same way as shoji do in a traditional Japanese house. Draw draperies are another practical way to shut off an area. The traverse rods can be mounted right on the ceiling. Tiebacks—decorative draperies that you don't actually close—may be used to further accentuate the demarcation line between a dining alcove and the rest of a living room, when you don't really wish or need to shut the dining area off completely.

More utilitarian but harder to move than screens are shelf units. You can choose between the open look of backless units, through which you see the other half of the room, and those with solid backs. Open shelves look fine rising all the way to the ceiling, but solid-backed models may appear too heavy. If you choose solid units, shop around first, and be sure that the backs are properly finished. Etagères, in the unfailingly popular chrome or brass and glass combination, offer a transparent version of open shelving that lets in the maximum amount of light while it divides.

BUILDING A WALL

Then there's the last and most expensive option: building a new wall or a partial wall to divide a room. Though heavy-duty construction is not really the subject of this book, if creating two rooms from one is your aim, here are a few things to be aware of before you begin:

- The space in question must be big enough to subdivide. Remember, you need more than just the space for the two new rooms. You must take into account the precious inches the wall itself is going to consume as well as any hallway that may be needed to provide access to one or both of the rooms. If you decide to add a closet, more square footage must be subtracted.
- The original space should have a double window so that each room may retain half, or, better still, two windows so that the new rooms will have sufficient light and air.
- The wall you erect must be as solid and soundproof as possible, otherwise it's not worth having.

You may prefer to extend an existing wall to create an alcove, a less extensive undertaking than building a complete wall. This can be accomplished by closing off all but a "doorway" into the short leg of an L-shaped room. This space can then become an office, a dining nook, a guest room, or a small den/TV room. In a room without any jogs or indentations to close off, a proscenium wall can create an alcove. The wall is erected a few feet from the exterior wall, which creates the alcove, and the opening is fitted with draw draperies or folding doors. When desired, the curtains or doors are opened and the two areas are reunited.

You might also consider a half-wall, say four feet high, which will

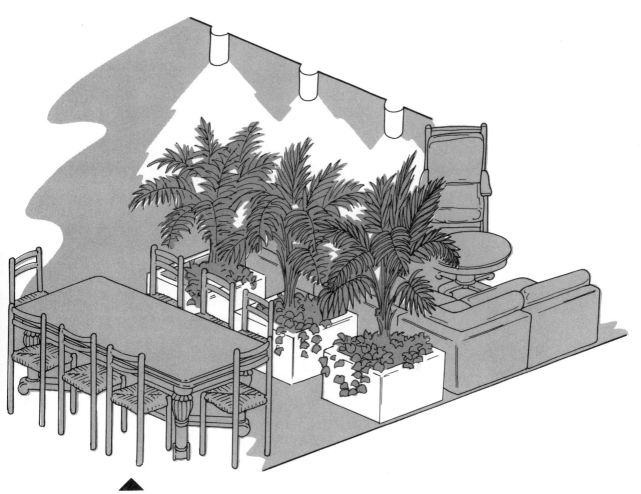

Teamed with ceiling-mounted plant lights, greenery can be a particularly attractive divider. Large, tree-like plants, such as ficus, schefflera, and palm, divide a room effectively when massed together. Oversized terra-cotta planters or wooden tubs are available to replace the not particularly sightly plastic containers these plants usually come in. An old trick but a good one is a display of small plants on the rungs of an open stepladder or on top of cubes of varying sizes. Adequate lighting, besides enhancing the divider, is essential if the plants are to remain healthy; a lot of scrawny branches or yellowing leaves will seriously compromise the lush look you're seeking.

screen almost anything on the other side and allow light and air to pass over the top. This kind of wall is frequently used to separate a kitchen from a dining area or a living room from a hallway.

Anything more elaborate cries out for professional help. We've all seen those glamorous photos of rooms with multilevel platforms, partial walls, columns, and so on in decorating magazines. In the hands of an amateur it may look as if you've erected a series of tombstones in your living room.

3 LIVING ROOMS WITH MORE

When you have a room that's not a family room, not a den, and not a dining room, what you have is a living room that needs a psychiatrist. In some new houses they're calling this living room/whatchamacallit combination the great room. But great for whom?

Traditionally, the living room has been the showpiece of a house. It's the room in which you invest a large proportion of your decorating dollars, the room you want to look as good as it possibly can. But when the living room has many demands on it, when it must take a beating day in and day out, it's difficult to reconcile your image of what a living room *should be* with what it really *is.*

In most multipurpose living rooms, the need to function as a family center comes first. Sometimes dining facilities must be there too. In addition, the living room is the primary place for entertaining and sometimes for putting up guests as well. No matter how you look at it, that's a large order to fill.

LIVING ROOM/FAMILY ROOM

When there are children in the picture, a living room/family room combination is likely to be your first priority. If you need to incorporate a play area for smaller children, try to isolate it by the furniture arrangement. Concentrate the adult conversation area at one end of the room and turn the space at the other end over to play. For instance, an L-shaped sofa grouping could face away from the children's area so that the kids play behind the couch.

A good way to keep children off the furniture is to make the floor a desirable play space. Do it with durable, wall-to-wall carpeting in a soil-resistant fiber and a nubby or tweedy texture that hides dirt. A small area rug in a busy, soil-concealing pattern, such as an Oriental, helps define the play area and will relieve the floor or the wall-to-wall carpeting underneath of wear and tear. A few large floor pillows with zippered covers invite floor-level lounging and the removable covers make them easy to keep clean.

Another way to keep children off the grown-up furniture is to give them furniture of their own. Child-sized stools, rocking chairs, and armchairs can be incorporated into the arrangement. One way to do this is to make sure your cocktail table is high enough for the children's chairs or stools to slip under; the cocktail table then becomes a practical place for children to work or eat. Just make sure you choose an indestructible surface like Formica for the table top.

If you can't keep the children off the furniture consider slip-covering sofas and chairs that are in continuous, hard use. When it comes to cleaning, no amount of fabric protector and upholstery shampoo can compare with the ease of taking a cover off and washing it. Of course, slipcovers must be made of colorfast and shrink-resistant fabric. And remember, you can remove them when the room is used for adult entertaining.

Another idea is using beanbag chairs. While at odds with traditional decor, they are at home with a more relaxed look. Beanbag chairs may not be elegant, but they are hardy and children seem to love them.

Where there are children, there are sure to be toys underfoot. Having a place to corral the blocks and stuffed animals can simplify your cleanup at the end of the day. If you're thinking about buying a wall unit, don't consider any style that doesn't have storage for toys. For example, a wall unit with closed cabinets on the bottom can hold bulky game boxes as well as smaller items that can be stored in plastic bins. Large, covered baskets that hold blocks or Lego pieces and a wooden toy chest that doubles as a coffee table are convenient and also attractive to look at. Colonial bench tables, with their storage compartment in the seat, and ottomans with removable tops make handy places for toys.

Since the TV is likely to be the focal point of a living room/family room—no matter what efforts you might make to the contrary—choose its location carefully. Don't put it where the seated watchers will block an essential traffic route or interfere with a conversation group. Beware of big console models; you're paying a lot of money for fancy cabinetry that isn't worth it esthetically and consumes a lot of valuable space. It's better to stash a portable TV in a wall unit that can hold a lot of other things as well, or in an armoire, which permits you to close the door on the tube.

DINING IN YOUR LIVING ROOM

Most living room/dining rooms work best when divided into separate but decoratively related spheres. Area rugs, étagères, plants, track lighting,

A comfortable conversation grouping and a floor-to-ceiling wall unit are all that is needed for relaxed family living in the room shown here. The wall unit has been finished with a soffit and moldings and appears to be built in. It takes care of storage for the TV, stereo, records, books, and games while allowing space for purely decorative objects like plants, plates, and ginger jars. The closed cabinets below the open shelves are handy for toy storage if needed. The round table in the foreground could be used for dining in a pinch and is perfect for card games and jigsaw puzzles. It could be covered with a round tablecloth for entertaining.

▶ Living room, office, and library can coexist peacefully if you adopt the "space within a space" technique. Here seating takes over the center of the room, and more functional elements the perimeter. The work area includes two pairs of lateral files (much less officey-looking than the standard type), a space for the typewriter, an ample flat work surface, and a storage cabinet for office supplies. The white laminate used throughout the office area reappears on the two cubes in the seating arrangement, effectively tying the room together. In the center the sofa and loveseat are placed at right angles. With the facing lounge chair the arrangement seats five comfortably.

and so on (see Chapter 2, "Dividing Lines") will increase the separate but equal feeling, as will the right furniture arrangement. For example, turn the backs of the sofa and/or chairs to the dining area, or elevate the area on a platform. In an L-shaped living room the short leg of the L is frequently an ideal spot for a table and chairs.

No matter how separate you'd like the two areas to appear, keep them in tune decoratively. This could mean using the same fabric on the dining

room chair seats that you used for throw pillows on the sofa, or choosing a cocktail and dining table in the same style or material—e.g., both glass and chrome, both mission oak, or both white Parsons.

Exactly what kind of dining facilities are required in a living room depends on whether eating there is an everyday or an occasional affair. If you don't have to have a table and chairs standing at the ready, there are quite a few alternatives to TV trays. Begin by making your coffee table

work for you. Small informal groups can dine Japanese style on floor cushions placed around a large low Parsons table. The traditional butler's coffee table has two drop leaves that can be opened up for dining. Some people, however, are uncomfortable seated on the floor. If you prefer to eat sitting on the sofa, choose a coffee table that is slightly higher than the norm so you don't have to bend over so far to reach the food. There are tables that come in this new "Continental" height, or you could make your own with a slab of marble or other material and stock legs from the lum-

A living room/dining room is difficult to arrange if the space is limited. One solution is to incorporate the dining area into the conversational group. Comfortable upholstered chairs (or any chairs that aren't too dining-roomy looking) are essential if you wish to carry this arrangement off. Here, wicker armchairs are pulled up to a glass-topped table placed close enough to the sofa for everyone to talk comfortably when the table isn't being used for dining. And the table works just as well for cocktails or for playing cards as it does for dinner. When drinks are finished and dinner is served, simply bring in dinner on a rolling cart, which remains to serve as a buffet.

beryard. While glass-topped coffee tables are good in small rooms because they appear to take up less space, from a double-duty standpoint they are not as satisfactory, since they have few storage options. One way to make a glass and chrome model earn its place in your living room is to make sure you can eat on it comfortably when you want to.

If coffee table dining holds only modest appeal, have a fold-down leaf built into a wall unit (many ready-made wall units come equipped with this option) or add one to an already existing bookcase. A fold-down leaf can accommodate two or three people for a meal while it doubles as a desk or a spot for a friendly game of checkers. For meals on the run, a set of nesting tables, instead of the customary end table, eliminates rickety tray tables from your life. More elegant is a skirted table topped with a fabric square, a round of glass, and/or placemats to protect the skirt. Other possibilities include a desk that you can clear quickly or a sofa table—Parsons style or drop leaf; side chairs can be quickly pulled into place for dining.

If your house is without a dining room and the kitchen is too small, eating in the living room isn't an alternative, it's a necessity. For everyday dining you're probably going to want a real table and chairs, especially if the family numbers more than two. You might consider a drop-leaf table because it folds down and is out of the way when not needed; a refectory-type or Parsons table that can be pushed against the wall for seating on one side and both ends or pulled out when more people must be seated; a round pedestal table that has no legs to maneuver around (an advantage) but cannot be placed flush against the wall (a disadvantage); a traditional dining room table with leaves to expand it when necessary; a bench table that becomes a seat; or a tip-top table with a top that can be flipped back against the wall (much the same idea).

PARTIES AND DINNER PARTIES: HOW TO FIT IT ALL IN

When entertaining is the order of the day, here are a few suggestions on how you can dramatically and inexpensively expand the options of a multipurpose living room.

If you need to accommodate a large number of people at a sit-down dinner but your everyday table seats only a few, keep a couple of collapsible sawhorses stacked in the closet. Topped with boards, a silence cloth, and linens, sawhorses can become an instant banquet table. Only the size of your room will limit the length of this "groaning board," which has been around at least since the Middle Ages.

Expand the seating capacity of a small round table by putting another larger plywood round on top. Of course, you'll need to make a bigger skirt to fit the new top, or you can buy a standard-size circular cloth. The extra round can be stored under a bed between uses. The same technique will

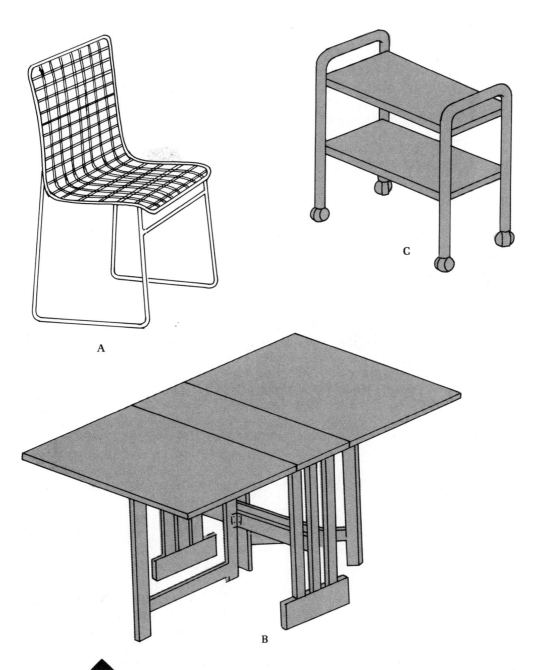

A

B

C

(A) Look for stackable chairs, like this one in wire grid, that can be easily stashed away until needed for dinner parties or entertaining. (B) Many manufacturers offer tables, such as this drop-leaf model, that take up only a few inches of depth when the leaves are folded down. (C) A rolling cart is a versatile accessory that can be a bar or a buffet when you're partying and a magazine rack or TV stand when you're not.

work on top of a square table and will vastly increase the numbers of diners that can be accommodated. (There is always room for one more at a round table, a sage hostess has said.) Just make sure the table you're using as a base is large enough to keep the new top from tipping to one side or the other and smashing all your Waterford at the same time.

If you must always drag the card table out of a closet before sitting down to a cozy dinner party or a few hands of bridge, make a handkerchief table part of your decor. A handkerchief table is a small square table with a leaf that folds down on the diagonal. It fits beautifully into a corner and can be pulled out and set up in seconds.

Your living room accessories should be enlisted along with the furniture; so fill the Chinese bowl with pretzels, the Shaker box with candy, and the faience vase with breadsticks. Press the credenza top, the sofa table, or the dining room table into service as a buffet.

The venerable campaign bar—a tray set on top of what looks like a collapsible luggage rack—is a good idea for a living room that lacks a bar. The tray and stand usually come in a set and are available in all price ranges, from lightweight mail order models to the finest mahogany trimmed with brass. Besides, if Napoleon made do with one, why can't

◀ This living room/dining room must also be used for business meetings by illustrator Robert Penny. With the help of designer Scott Kemper, he's found a flexible arrangement in his minimalist fashion. The loveseat, which he "upholstered" with a painter's drop cloth, is angled into the wall to focus on the window, which opens on a spectacular view. Penny has hidden his stereo speakers under three canvas squares and uses them as pedestals for accessories—today an art deco clock or bowl of fruit, tomorrow something new. The dining room table is of the institutional metal variety—painted black—but the campy lamp on top of it attracts all the attention. A miscellany of chairs commutes between the dining and seating areas. Note that there's not a hint of a bed glimpsed through the open door. Two metal cabinets used as the headboard obscure it completely, so the door can be left open even during business conferences.

you? Between parties you could use the tray on top of a chest or low stand for a coffee table, or, if it's particularly good looking, as a decorative accent on a sideboard or propped against the wall.

For another impromptu bar—one that's particularly useful for large parties at which you may want to have more than one place to serve drinks—have a piece of Masonite cut to fit the top of a desk, table, or dresser. (It's cheap and easy to find at the lumberyard.) Cover it with a cloth and then set up the bottles, glassware, and ice bucket without worrying that the finish on your good furniture will be damaged. If the tablecloth is floor length, you can stash extra booze underneath.

Rolling carts make handy all-in-one bars, so if you have one that is normally used for something else, commandeer it during the festivities. You can also load it with mousses, tortes, and gâteaux as they do in France and close your dinner party with an impressive *chariot de desserts.* You might clear some book shelves of their weighty tomes and fill the space temporarily with bottles of holiday cheer as well as rows of sparkling glassware.

WHEN THE LIVING ROOM IS FOR SLEEPING

If your living room must also serve as a guest room, there are lots of directions in which to go. The most traditional solution, and probably the simplest, is to make a sleep sofa or convertible chair part of your seating arrangement. Convertible sofas have come a long way since the first cave man unrolled his bear skin. Improved mechanisms have made couches with fold-away mattresses easier to operate. Better mattress and spring systems provide firmer support for a sounder night's sleep. It's possible to purchase sleep sofas in a huge variety of styles from colonial to art deco to twenty-first century. Most modular systems offer at least one convertible element as well. The convertible sofa, however, is only part of the story. There are all kinds of ways, orthodox and otherwise, to make room for visitors in your living room. Turn to Chapter 9, "The Guesting Game," for more details.

EASY UPKEEP

Remember that a living room that must be all things at all times needs periodic refurbishing, no matter what you do. Any move to channel some traffic into another area of your home will help make the living room a more pleasant and relaxing place to be. Just don't let things go so to pieces that you face major redecorating instead of a patch-up job every few years.

To distribute wear and tear more evenly on your furniture, experiment with different arrangements. Keep things moving around. Rotate the rug, change from winter to summer slipcovers, put away heavy winter draperies and hang up inexpensive matchstick blinds or summery roman shades you can make quite easily. You'll find your winter rugs and curtains will last longer and retain their color better if they're not subjected to months of summer sunshine. If you have space to store them, you could even roll up your wool rugs and put down straw matting in the warm season. The price of replacing a fine rug or lined draperies far exceeds the cost of these summer substitutes.

Walls resist soiling longer if they are painted with an eggshell or semi-gloss finish instead of flat. Woodwork should always be painted in semi-gloss or high-gloss enamel. Mend small rents in wallpaper and paste down loose corners right away to circumvent the tendency present in all of us to peel it a little more!

4 DOUBLE-DUTY DINING ROOMS

The dining room is one of the best candidates for double-duty decorating because it's occupied at such predictable hours and because those hours are usually so few and far between. So far between that sometimes months pass since your last dinner party. But even if your dining room is used every day, it's perfectly possible to keep the room for eating and still combine it with other activities. After all, there's no law that states if you have a table and chairs in the dining room, you're allowed only a sideboard or a breakfront to go with them. So toss out the rigid requirements of the formal dining room and try on some flexible combinations to see how they suit you.

THE DINING ROOM/MUSIC ROOM

If there's an up-and-coming Liberace in the family, fit the piano into the dining room floor plan. A grand piano does consume a considerable amount of space, but spinets and uprights are much easier to find room for. (Keep a lookout for "apartment-size" pianos, scaled to fit smaller spaces.) The lid of the piano can serve as a buffet—when properly protected from hot serving dishes—and don't forget the candelabra. Musical accessories such as brass music stands, antique scores, a violin framed in a shadow box, or a bust of Beethoven could then set the tone for the overall decorating scheme. Almost any instrument (with the possible exception of a drum and cymbals set or a lot of electric rock music equipment) adds a cultivated feeling to an otherwise ordinary dining room.

DINING ROOM/LIBRARY

A book-lined dining room has a cozy, clubby air that's quite in keeping with the relaxed atmosphere you want for dining. You could go conservative with dark-toned walls and book shelves stained deep mahogany. An easy chair or two, with reading lamps and an attractive bookstand, wouldn't be out of place, nor would a brass chandelier over the dining room table.

You needn't stick totally with the men's club look either. You can achieve quite another feeling, lighter and brighter, and still make all those books look right at home in the dining room. You might paint the room white and allow the books to be the most important decorating elements, particularly if you have lots of hard-cover books or sets of classics in elegant bindings.

Add a few modern prints by Calder or Picasso—posters will do as well—and a sculptural dining room table with some modernistic chairs. In this kind of environment, the sideboard could be a contemporary Parsons desk where you work the majority of the time. Add one touch of glitter with a crystal chandelier over the dining room table, or a taste of the rustic with a black, wrought-iron one with real candles.

DINING ROOM/SITTING ROOM/GUEST ROOM

Combine your dining room with a sitting room by adding a sofa and chairs that blend with the style of your dining room furniture. There are several reasons for doing this. If your main seating area in the living room also contains the TV or is right next to the children's play area, it's nice to create a peaceful haven that is purely for adults. By adding a seating area to the dining room, you make more comfortable spots for guests to perch during a buffet dinner. A dining room/sitting room can also serve as a good place for a cocktail before dinner or for coffee afterward. Should you be short of space for an overnight guest, choose a convertible chair or loveseat as part of the sitting room grouping. It's a welcome change from the foldout bed in the living room that everyone is forever tripping over in the middle of the night.

DINING ROOM/PLAY ROOM

In houses built before the 1960s, when the family room hadn't yet been invented, finding an indoor play area for children is a problem. The dining room, in most cases located near the kitchen, is the logical candidate for the job. It's best to choose a dining table that folds out of the way during

Dramatize your dining room, and divide it at the same time. Note that the platform must be large enough to hold the table and chairs with room to spare—you don't want to push yourself away from the table and fall over the edge. To create a den, two wall units face each other across the lower level of the room, with a TV tucked among the mementos and books in the wall unit (not shown here). The seating consists of two armless upholstered chairs that can be easily rearranged. A stack of floor pillows serves as an ottoman; dismantled, the pillows become extra seats on the floor.

the day and has a surface that is tough enough to survive finger paints and model airplane glue. There's a durable clear plastic film available by the yard in houseware stores that is perfect for protecting the table or a section of floor where an easel is set up or another messy activity is going on. Dining room furniture, other than the table and chairs, should be selected with toy storage in mind. If the dining room has a closet, turn it over to toy storage for now and reclaim it later. A paneled screen will also conceal toys, such as a tricycle or slide, that are too large for the closet or cupboard. A banquette, built the length of one of the dining room walls, adds more storage space if you hinge the seats. Not only will the children have a place to sprawl, but so will dinner guests at large buffets. The floor remains a problem in any room that doubles for play. Bare floors are cold and can be unwelcoming, so carpeting is recommended.

Keep it in some practical, soil-disguising color—not too light or too dark—or in a busy pattern such as an Oriental or a geometric.

DINING ROOM/TV ROOM/GAME ROOM

If you're tired of eating Sunday dinner alone because the Steelers have first and goal on the Ram 6, why not give in and get a second TV for the dining room? You can hide a portable in the china cabinet and bring it out as needed, or make it a part of a dining room wall unit. With comfortable seating at one end of the room or with a banquette arrangement instead of a traditional table and chairs, the room will be used much more frequently. In fact, it will assume the role of game room, an ideal spot for playing cards and games, doing jigsaw puzzles, or pursuing any kind of activity that demands a flat work surface.

THE DINING ROOM/OFFICE

Since the dining room is used at such predictable times, it is an ideal candidate for an at-home work space. Frequently, it's a bit off the beaten track in the layout of the house, a definite advantage if you're doing serious work that demands peace and quiet. There are all kinds of ways to combine an office with your dining room, many of which are dealt with in Chapter 8, "Working at Home." Briefly, here are three basic ways the office/dining room combination can be made to work.

First, you can simply make one area of your dining room into an office by adding a desk that harmonizes with the rest of the furniture in the room. In a dining room filled with golden oak, for instance, an oak roll-top desk would be an ideal choice because the front closes on the disorder. A drop-front secretary also can be shut and would fit perfectly into a room filled with eighteenth-century originals or reproductions.

Next, you can create an alcove with curtains, screens, blinds, or partitions so the office can be closed off when the room is used for dining. This way it won't matter much what's behind the divider since the office area is going to be hidden most of the time anyway.

Another alternative is to take over a wall and design a unit that would accommodate all your office needs. You could put one together from ready-made components or have one custom built. Either way the unit should include file cabinets, a work surface, storage cabinets, a phone, a typewriter, book shelves, and anything else that you need for your work. Much of it could be disguised by cabinet doors decorated with moldings or mirrors to blend with your dining room decor.

DINING ROOM/STORAGE ROOM

Every family has a number of awkward items to store—everyday things like the ironing board and vacuum cleaner and exotic ones like lacrosse sticks and fly rods—and frequently no place to put them. In much the same way that you can add an office in an alcove to your dining room, you can create a storage room. An easy and inexpensive method is to curtain across one end of the dining room, leaving two or three feet between the draperies and the wall. You can easily stash a couple of bicycles, all of your suitcases, and even your ex-husband's college trophies back there. More elaborate would be to build a permanent partition that would enable you to use the new wall as a support for shelves or hanging rods, and might even create a couple of new closets.

An office in the dining room doesn't have to interfere when it's hidden, most of the time anyway, behind a set of draw draperies. A two-foot partition was built at right angles to the wall on both sides of the room, creating an alcove; shelves, cubbyholes, and cabinets were installed in this new space. The opening is spanned with a wooden rod from which draperies are hung on matching wooden rings. To make the office area blend with the dining room, an old Victorian table is used for a desk. But since the office disappears, it's not really necessary to invest in any expensive pieces.

An attractive alternative to the single-purpose dining room—and one that fits neatly into "country" style—is the dining room/keeping room. A keeping room, which in colonial days really functioned as the kitchen, was usually furnished with rustic tables, a sideboard, perhaps a settle, gathered around the hearth. Today you can achieve this look with antique or reproduction pieces: a couple of wing or rush-bottomed chairs or a bench table that converts from table to seat and also has a handy storage compartment in the base. If you don't have a fireplace, you can fake one with an old mantel or install a woodburning stove which will guarantee that the family will congregate here on chilly days. Shiny copper warming pans, salt-glazed stoneware, pewter mugs, and blue-and-white plates are all possible accessories.

5 BETTER BEDROOMS

Getting more out of your master bedroom can mean combining it with an office or an art studio or anything else that suits your way of life. Even when it's not necessary to have the bedroom function as two rooms in one, it still makes sense to create a bedroom that offers more than a place to lay your head from 11 to 7.

BEDROOM/SITTING ROOM

A natural extension of the bedroom is the bedroom/sitting room, a room where you can read, study, or talk during the day. Very little furniture needs to be added to the average master bedroom to create this hybrid. A skirted table is a logical acquisition. It can be used as a desk, as an informal dining table, or as a make-up table (with the addition of a glass top), and can conceal storage underneath. Use one in place of a bedside table. To make the skirted table idea even more flexible, you can mount a file cabinet on casters, then top it with a plywood round. The entire table then moves from place to place at the touch of a finger.

If you're going to use the bedroom for more than sleeping or taking naps, it's essential to have someplace other than the bed to sit down. A chaise longue is ideal for the bedroom. It looks like it belongs there, particularly if there's a lamp and a basket of magazines or your needlepoint nearby. You may prefer a club chair and matching ottoman, which are less bedroomy looking but just as comfortable as a chaise. A bit more formal is a loveseat that could be joined by a side chair if you have the

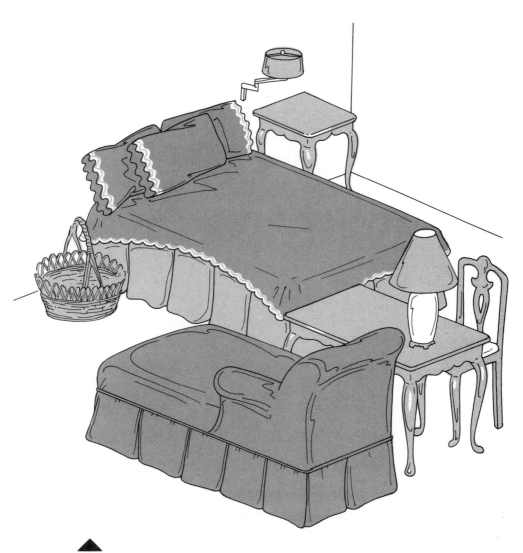

One of the easiest ways to get more mileage out of your bedroom is to make it into a sitting room as well—not to be confused with a "bedsitter," which in England means studio apartment. Mothers and fathers often need a place to escape that is not part of the children's stamping grounds. The arrangement shown here works beautifully, even in a small space, and has a somewhat European flavor. The chaise is positioned next to the desk so that one lamp will do for both, and there's a place to perch your cup of tea while you're reading the Sunday paper. Two people can converse comfortably, one flopped down on the bed and the other relaxing on the chaise. The wall-mounted lamp leaves the bedside table free for other things. Note that the only strictly bedroom piece is the bed; the rest of the furniture can move into other rooms. There's no need for a bureau since the closet has been made so efficient you don't need one.

space. Make sure there's proper lighting for reading, sewing, etc., so that the seating is as functional as it is decorative.

A built-in window seat brings you closer to the out-of-doors and is ideal for someone who doesn't mind curling up her legs. Cover the cushions with the fabric coordinate of the wallpaper, the sheet pattern, or an old patchwork quilt, and pile the seat with handmade pillows.

A recessed window has other possibilities too. If a window seat isn't your cup of tea, you can fill in the space with book shelves or bridge the gap with a desk top or a dressing table.

At the foot of the bed an upholstered bench or blanket chest with a cushion on top provides that necessary spot to perch when you're getting dressed. A carpeted ledge that wraps around the bed frame serves the same function just as well and has a very contemporary flavor. Other helpful additions to a bedroom/sitting room include a small drop-front secretary that closes up to hide the litter of bills and a table—Parsons or drop-leaf—that can be put to a variety of uses.

BEDROOM/AUDIOVISUAL CENTER

If you tend to avoid your bedroom because it lacks a TV or stereo, include space for your audio and video needs when you plan the decor. Instead of a portable television perched precariously on a rickety TV table, find a spot where the set can be viewed in comfort but where it doesn't create an unsightly mess of wire. You might consider putting it in a blanket chest at the foot of the bed and taking it out when desired, or making it part of a wall unit with its own set of louvered doors. Think about building the TV set into the bottom of a marble-topped washstand or even hiding it in a sleek, wall-mounted, two-door cabinet. The large screen of a projection television could be concealed behind a pair of draw draperies.

If you crave the strains of André Kostelanetz you could import them via remote speakers located in another room, but this can be inconvenient if you want to listen to music before you drop off to sleep. You might prefer to keep a compact AM/FM radio/cassette player on your bedside table or hidden in a bedside cabinet. An armoire or any kind of doored cabinet would conceal all your audio needs and a TV as well.

Many audio and video enthusiasts love the way all these electronic gizmos look and would rather flaunt their amplifiers, turntables, tape decks, and headphones than hide them in a closet. However, there's a world of difference between a muddle of wires and components atop a dresser and a nifty, futuristic, all-in-one audio-video center. Quite a few manufacturers have come up with attractive units that organize every piece of decibel-producing equipment you'll ever want. In a high-tech room you could stow it all on those wire grid shelves you can find at most houseware stores.

An inexpensive way to create an alcove bed when you haven't got an alcove is to make one out of partitions and draperies. Two plywood panels, one at either end of the bed (here an antique sleigh bed), create a cozy nook. The "walls" of the alcove can be wallpapered, covered with fabric, or even upholstered for a luxurious look (fabric is stapled over a layer of batting). A nice extra is that by building the alcove, you've added what amounts to two more closets to the room. One could be fitted with shelves and the other with a hanging rod. Note: The baffle that bridges the space is flush to the ceiling and reinforces the recessed feeling.

BEDROOM/GYM

With the current fitness craze going forward unabated, it's now possible to turn your boudoir into a Nautilus center. This can be extremely advantageous, since sticking to a daily routine of sit-ups and other tortures requires more discipline than most of us possess. Make it as easy on yourself as possible by having everything you need right at hand. With little disruption your bedroom can become a pleasant place to sit up, chin up, pull up, or otherwise get into shape.

Even in a bedroom that is used primarily for sleeping, it's still practical, indeed preferable, to turn one corner into a private place for napping, reading, embroidering, and the like. In this bedroom (the author's own), adding a chaise made all the difference. It provides a place to flop down and relax, sparing wear and tear on the bedspread, and unwinding on the chaise doesn't seem like such a complete collapse as getting into bed. The armoire is mostly filled with clothes but one side conceals the TV, which can be viewed from both the bed and the chaise. The room also provides a lot of storage—in the armoire, under the high fourposter, and in the blanket chest at the foot of the bed. If necessary, you could even make use of the space under the skirted table.

If you do ballet exercises, install a ballet barre on the wall or, even better, on a mirrored wall. Not only can the mirror be used for dressing, but it will help open up and brighten a small room. For floor exercises and stretching, keep an exercise mat rolled up at the foot of your bed. It looks like a quilt and, besides being better for your back, is much more pleasant than a bare floor or synthetic carpet to work out on. For doing chin-ups or pull-ups, you can buy one of those expandable exercise bars. They are pressure mounted, no screws are needed, and they fit inside a doorway or a closet door frame. Just be careful that you have enough room so you're not bumping into hangers or the tie rack when you chin up. Note: This item is often found in children's mail-order catalogues. It's inexpensive and kids love it.

Storing all your exercise gear in one place, such as inside your closet door, makes the fitness routine easier. Hang your leotard and jump rope on colorful plastic hooks or stuff everything in a laundry bag, a basket, or a couple pockets in your shoe bag. Small weights for stretching routines can be stored in wire grid containers mounted on the door. Light barbells are usually sold with a rack that can find a home in the bottom of a closet. An exercycle is a fairly weighty item so you're not going to want to move it around a lot. If you don't want to look at it all the time, put it in the corner and hide it behind a folding screen. The same goes for a running machine (Didn't it used to be called a treadmill?) and the various types of weightlifting machines. Heavy weights for bench pressing require special equipment that usually cannot be supported by the floor of an average home. The basement is the only suitable location for this kind of activity. Easier to store are small trampolines designed for running in place; they can fit in the bottom of the closet or under the bed.

SOUND AND LIGHT IN THE BEDROOM

For the occasional catnap, not to mention more sleep at night, decorate your bedroom with soundproofing in mind. This goes double for those who like their music at deafening levels, but in that case it's the neighbors' sleep you're concerned about. The thing to remember is that hard, bare surfaces absorb less sound than soft, porous ones. By using sound-absorbing materials in your bedroom you will lessen the sound that goes out as well as the noise that comes in.

Outside, install double-glazed windows or storm windows to help reduce the amount of street noise that reaches your ears, an important consideration in the city. Double windows also will save a significant amount of energy by keeping the air conditioning (in summer) and the heat (in winter) from escaping.

Inside, draperies can cut off a good deal of unwanted sound while—like the windows—they help reduce your energy costs. To be most effective draperies should be lined; there are special fabrics on the market that are made to do the job. Quilted draperies, sometimes called window quilts, also are popular as sound and heat insulators.

Wall-to-wall carpeting with a thick layer of padding underneath deadens sound in a room and helps keep noise from penetrating to the floor below. (Most apartment dwellers will testify that a great deal of nuisance noise comes from the apartment above.) The insulating effect of wall-to-

If your clothes storage situation has passed the crisis point, you might consider curtaining off a twenty- to twenty-three-inch-deep strip down one side of the room (preferably a windowless wall) to make another closet. You could, in fact, hide a dressing table back there as well. The simplest way to go about it would be to run an expansion shower rod across the space. If the distance is too great, use ceiling-mounted curtain rods. For a more elaborate effect the drapery works could be hidden behind a cornice. Behind the draperies there would be room for shelves as well as hanging bars. Zippered garment bags could easily handle your out-of-season clothes.

wall carpeting can be increased by laying area rugs on top. All area rugs should have a pad underneath them, not just for the sound-deadening effect but to increase the lifetime of the rug.

For walls, fabric shirred on rods or stapled flat will absorb more sound than a coat of paint. Other possibilities are to cover the wall with cork, felt, or panel behind which you have installed, in this last case, a layer of insulation and allowed for air space. (Air space also reduces the ability of sound to carry.)

If it's necessary to soundproof your ceiling, you can choose from a variety of acoustical tile systems. Most you can install yourself, although many are too institutional looking for a bedroom. If you play the drums or the tuba and plan to do so in the bedroom, you may have to consider a professional soundproofing job, which could entail the expense of building a room within a room and is not really the subject here.

Lighting is important in a bedroom where you will be reading or doing office work as well as sleeping. If your bedroom does double duty, you should have two kinds of lighting: good direct light for working and softer

Illustrator Robert Penny's bedroom makes use of the furniture from his old studio apartment with the addition of a lamp, a new window treatment, and new carpeting. The layout, devised by designer Scott Kemper, floats the bed at an angle in the center of the room. The base of the bed is a couple of custom drawing cabinets which Penny needs to store his work; the headboard is two old gray steel office cabinets—they hold books, work materials, bedding, clothes, and an exercise mat. The television stands on a tubular rolling car that Penny pirates for other purposes—a bar or portable buffet in the living room. Pleated window shades are mounted to pull down the top so that light can stream in from the top. Penny hangs artwork on transparent fish line attached to the ceiling molding since he likes to change things around frequently. In fact, his apartment is never the same two visits running.

mood lighting for relaxing. The light from a ceiling fixture is never satisfactory, so a good reading lamp next to the bed and one close to an easy chair are absolutely necessary. When your desk is in the bedroom, you'll need a desk lamp, too.

If you're short of space, a wall-mounted lamp that swivels or an artist's lamp on a long, flexible arm works fine next to the bed. Small apothecary lamps are versatile, sit on the floor, and can be tucked almost anywhere. In general, incandescent bulbs are preferable to fluorescent ones, which may hum and have a way of making most people look sick. Track lights are a bit glary but could be used with wall washers to set a mood. Think about having a master switch installed next to the bed so you can turn off the whole shebang without moving.

6 COMBINATION KITCHENS

Once upon a time, the kitchen was the central room of the house. People not only cooked and ate there, they did practically everything else there, too. Over the years, the kitchen became specialized and isolated, relegated in most houses solely to food preparation. As this happened, the kitchen grew smaller and more utilitarian; it became less of a gathering place for people and more of a comglomeration of appliances.

Today the trend has reversed. Once again family and friends are congregating in the kitchen to schmooze with the cook, to dine on homemade pasta, and to drink cappuccino. The new American fascination with good food and good cooking means that houses and apartments with large kitchens are prized, that kitchen renovations are as numerous as brands of gourmet mustard, and that the restaurant stove and the Cuisinart have replaced the twenty-four-inch color TV and the Eames chair as status symbols.

THE REMODELING QUESTION

Remodeling a kitchen cannot be undertaken lightly. It's a big job, the kind that usually requires a great deal of planning and a considerable outlay of money. If what you have in mind is more complicated than a change of wallpaper or new linoleum, it's best to call in an expert to advise you. Before you sit down with him or her, make a list of what you do—and don't—want in your new kitchen. Naturally, not everything will be possible, so it's going to be a question of what's most important to you.

Sometimes an original kitchen contains enough floor space for your plans, but frequently the only way to find the square footage you need is to tear down a wall or two. Depending on the layout of your house or apartment, you might combine the kitchen with the dining room, a porch, an old pantry, a maid's room, a hallway, or even a carport or garage—in short, any other adjacent area that could contribute more as part of the kitchen than it does on its own.

The combined space must then be distributed among cooking, dining, and/or living areas, plus any others you wish to incorporate (pet shelter, entertainment center, etc.). Call in an expert to help you decide where you want things to go, working within the limitations of your space, your wiring, and your plumbing. Yes, wiring and plumbing. Installing a special 220-volt circuit or moving pipes and gas lines adds enormously to the expense of redoing a kitchen. You should weigh all the alternatives before you bring in fancy new electrical equipment or relocate the stove or the sink.

In any case, your aim is to create a compact but convenient food preparation area in one part of the room so you can devote the rest to living, dining, or whatever else you've decided on. A work island, a peninsula-shaped counter, open shelving, and built-in seating all draw demarcation lines between the kitchen space and those areas designated for other things (see illustrations). The decorating scheme will play an important part in making the finished room a well-integrated one, not just a kitchen with a sofa or a dining table in it.

KITCHEN CHARACTER

A kitchen where more than cooking is done should have a look and a personality that go beyond its utilitarian purpose. For example, instead of going bananas over cabinets—a roomful of wall-to-wall and floor-to-ceiling models can be overwhelming—replace some of them with open shelving. This allows you to decorate with the things you use every day, such as rolling pins and cracker tins, jars of interestingly shaped noodles, jugs, pitchers, and mixing bowls. And don't be afraid to put antiques in the kitchen. After all, pie safes, corner cupboards, and plate racks were all meant to be in the kitchen, or nearby, in the first place. An armoire looks great in a kitchen and the inside can be used as a bar, a table-linen cabinet, or a storage place for canned goods or other foods.

An unnecessary touch, such as a skylight, will not only brighten a kitchen but also will provide it with an ideal spot for a hanging herb garden. Old-time wooden kitchen cabinets, the kind with lots of little panes of glass, can be salvaged, stripped, and worked in with modern cabinetry for a warmer, more eclectic look. Remember, however, that in the greasy kitchen environment you'll have to wash all those little windows frequently.

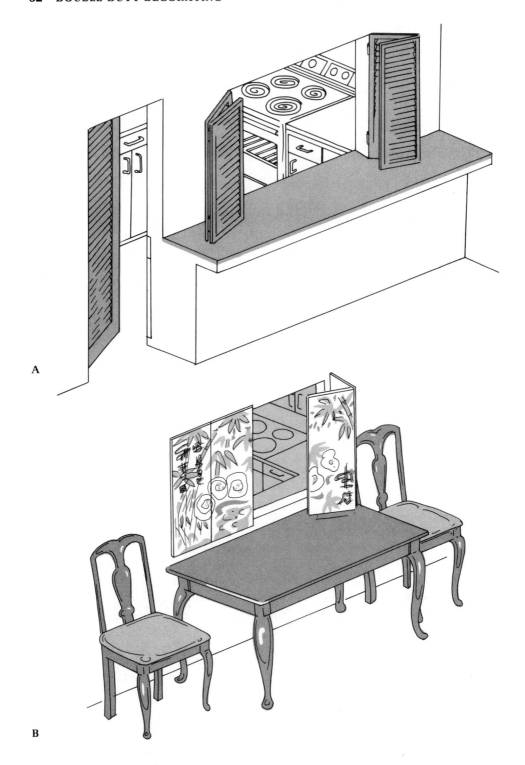

A

B

If your kitchen is inconveniently long, one end can be converted into a dining alcove and utility area with the addition of two built-in closets. Those pictured here are on either side of the window. (The open-work trim above the table is purely decorative.) The eating area seats four comfortably on benches that look like settles. A fifth seat could be added by placing a chair at the end of the table. The closets conceal a complete floor-to-ceiling pantry and a stackable washer/dryer combination. A glass top on the table reduces the number of times the cloth will have to be laundered.

A dining room pass-through adds the eat-in function to a kitchen where there isn't room for a table, and frees up almost the entire dining room for other uses. A pass-through is handy even in a traditional dining room where you could have an eating bar for quick meals during the day and a dining room table for dinner and formal occasions. The first illustration (A) shows an attractive yet utilitarian look. A counter has been built at bar stool height in the dining room. The opening for the pass-through can be closed off with louvered folding shutters. The second view (B) is a pass-through into a rather formal dining room. Here the opening is disguised with panels hand-painted in an oriental design, appropriately elegant. The table can be used as a sideboard or for dining *à deux*.

A peninsula arrangement works quite well combined with something more ambitious than a simple eating bar. In this kitchen/den/dining room a sizable circular table that seats four or five has been built right on the end of the peninsula. Above the peninsula, a row of ceiling-hung cabinets adds a considerable amount of storage space, but there's enough of an opening between them and the counter that a person seated at the table can see and easily converse with someone in the adjacent den. Unattractive necessities like the trash can be fit into their own section of cabinet under the counter.

If sleek and modern is more your style, cabinetry will be a very important factor in creating the look you want, so it's probably worth the extra money to invest in the best-designed cabinets you can afford. To complement the modern cabinetry, add a wall of polished cookware suspended from a stainless-steel grid, chrome hooks, or a pot rack, and hang more pots and utensils from the ceiling. Make sure that whatever furniture you choose for dining or lounging is in the same contemporary vein as the rest of the room.

Keep your counter tops spotless; whether your version of modern runs to super-sophisticated or high tech or somewhere in between, the secret to the contemporary look in kitchens is clean and uncluttered surfaces. One way to make this easier is to store all those small appliances—food processor, coffeemaker, blender, mixer, toaster oven, the list goes on and on—on open shelves or in cabinets directly above the work surface. Then each one can be lifted down and plugged into an outlet handily located in the splash.

All kitchens need at least one large drawer subdivided into roomy compartments to hold all the miscellaneous stuff like measuring cups, slotted spoons, can openers, spatulas, egg beaters, and the like. Wooden implements look great standing in earthenware crocks. If you're having a hood made for over the stove (by law you must if you wish to have an industrial stove in your home), the bottom lip will usually be designed so you can hang from it ladles, skimmers, and spatulas from a restaurant supply house.

Cooks with a compulsion to save grocery bags should break this bad habit. Not only are used bags a haven for roaches, as city dwellers know, but they leak and become greasy when used to line the trash can. No matter what gadget you get to hold them, they are bulky and unsightly. Use plastic bags instead.

THE EAT-IN KITCHEN

An eat-in kitchen should be more than a chipped dinette set next to the stove, particularly if you've sacrificed your formal dining room to the kitchen cause or if you eat in the kitchen every day. A table in the kitchen doesn't have to be a kitchen table. When space is limited, a drop-leaf table in maple or pine condenses itself just as well as a Formica model. Wood adds a warm country flavor, too. A narrow refectory table can be pushed against the wall day-to-day and pulled out when extra seating is needed. A laminated Parsons table or a sleek chrome and butcher block combo are more contemporary and can be made up in almost any size.

When there's not room for the table to be freestanding, it can be made a part of another structure, such as a work island or a peninsula, by adding a ledge or an L-shaped projection to it. Some manufacturers have even come up with eating surfaces that pull out from kitchen cabinets like drawers and then slide away after use.

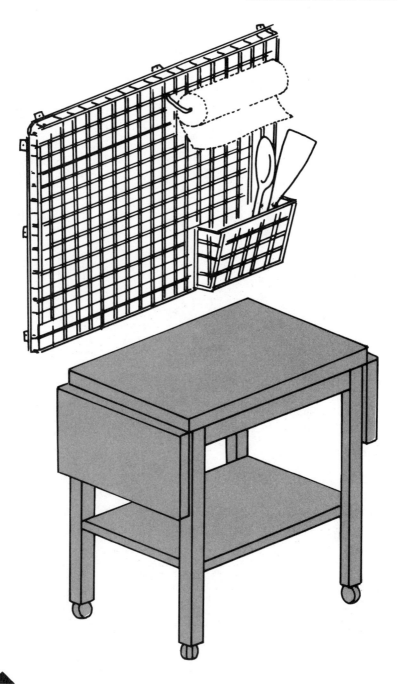

A butcher block-topped cart is a fine way to expand limited counter space in a small kitchen. It can be moved into the center of the room to act like a work island when needed. Above it a wire grid storage unit can hold all your rolls of food wrap, paper towels, and frequently used small utensils—whisks, spatulas, wooden spoons, can opener, and the like.

Even a tiny kitchen can offer more in the way of eating facilities than a stool at the sink. This kitchen has a banquette in the corner—with storage space in the bases, of course—and a triangular table topped with laminate that slides out to allow the diners in. The cushions have been slip-covered in gingham-checked vinyl so they are impervious to spills. The table supplies counter space, and the triangular shape allows traffic to pass by comfortably. The trash can has its own compartment under the counter next to the back door; not only is it not in view, it's not underfoot.

KITCHEN/FAMILY ROOM

If your kitchen is to be a family room, too, you might think about using a sleep sofa as your main piece of furniture. That way you'll end up with a triple-threat room: kitchen, family room, guest accommodations. If space is too constricted for a standard sofa, you can build a banquette that is quite comfortable to sit on when the seats and backs are padded. If the bases are hinged, the interior becomes auxiliary storage space. Naturally, the family room will have a TV, and now is the time to build it into the kitchen cabinetry, along with the stereo, bulky speakers, a video game

console, a home computer, etc. Think about designing one cabinet to store liquor and glasses. It will work fine as a bar when the door folds down for mixing drinks.

It's quite possible, and usually necessary, for a combination kitchen to include more than just the dining room or family room. There's no reason yours can't have at least one or more of the following:

- **Home office.** A work space where you pay bills, copy recipes, or make phone calls can be tucked into a corner or small section of counter space.

This rectangular kitchen has a peninsula that separates the cooking area from the rest of the room. One side of the peninsula serves as a dining bar for breakfast, lunch, and the occasional quick dinner. The other side, facing the refrigerator and stove, houses the sink and the dishwasher as well as cabinets for storage. Open shelving above offers ample space for everyday dishes and some ornamental items. It also reinforces the dividing line between the cooking and the living sides of the room, while allowing the cook to see and converse with people on the other side. Under the window, a banquette provides more seating with storage inside for infrequently used kitchen equipment and a record collection. The wall to the left (not shown) features kitchen cabinets with a built-in microwave oven, TV, and stereo. The sofa folds out to accommodate the occasional overflow guest. Note that the banquette area could have become a home office or a sewing center.

- *Laundry.* A stackable washer/dryer set doesn't take up much floor space, and the machines can be hidden behind louvered doors or ones that match your kitchen cabinetry. Front-loading, side-by-side models can be topped with a butcher block or a slab of the same material your counter tops are made of to function as additional counter space or an eating bar.
- *Workshop.* Keep the most frequently called on tools and home repair supplies close at hand by turning over part of a kitchen cabinet to hammers, screwdrivers, glue, touch-up paint, shade pulls, light bulbs, tile grout, weatherstripping, and the like.
- *Sewing center.* If you're a serious seamstress, it may be worth the expense to have your sewing machine installed in the kitchen. Have it built in just as you would a dishwasher or a trash compactor; a console sewing machine can be removed from its cabinet and reinstalled in a section of counter. A portable model can be stored behind cabinet doors below the area where it's going to be used.

7 STASHING THE KIDS

There are two kinds of kids' rooms—the kind you see in magazines and the real kind. Let's face it, most children's rooms aren't decorated, they just grow, like Topsy, and keep on growing. Children's toys and games come with millions of pieces, and unless you have a child who can keep his Legos separate from his collection of Star Wars figures, or her Barbie Doll wardrobe from getting mixed up with her Smurfs, you have to make allowances for more or less constant disorder. The young artist produces more finger paintings, pinch pots, and macaroni collages than could possibly be displayed in a lifetime. And don't forget the hockey pucks, skate keys, baseball bats, mimeographed messages from school, and arithmetic homework.

On top of this, many children today are sharing rooms, putting twice the strain on an already overcrowded space. When the children are of different sexes or greatly different ages you really have to divide whatever space you have into two distinct areas, even if you're starting with a twelve-by-fourteen-foot room.

THE BASICS PLUS A LITTLE EXTRA

Even children fortunate enough to have rooms of their own must usually do more than just sleep in them; there must be space for play and space for study. The first essential is sleeping accommodations—although not necessarily in the form of a standard bed—that will last from age two or three until adulthood or at least until age twelve, a good time to make the transition from childish decor to a more grown-up look. There should also

Classic bunk beds need not always be made of classic materials. These bunks are made of durable metal pipe painted bright red. Willy, the little boy who sleeps in this room, is the author's son. The upper bunk is for his overnight guests and for visits from his older sister, Jessie. On one wall, two matching cabinets and a hinged-top toy chest were built-in to compensate for the fact that Willy's closet is the laundry center. The top of either cabinet is exactly the right height for a changing table and can be used as such until the children no longer need it. The top of the toy chest is carpeted and, with more pillows, makes a comfortable window seat. When desk space is called for, the toy chest can be easily exchanged for a work surface. On the facing wall (not shown), a small chifforobe with drawers and hanging space takes care of all Willy's clothes. His stuffed animal collection sits on top. The upper bunk and the ladder are always the focus of some kind of play—frequently part of a hook and ladder truck. The center of the room has been left open for block building and a train set which pulls out from under the bed.

be a work surface with a stool or desk chair that adjusts to the child's height and enough open area on the floor to spread out the building blocks or build a pillow house. (As for other kinds of chairs, most kids don't really need them so you might as well save the space.) Toy and clothes storage spaces should be accessible so, theoretically, your child can clean up after himself.

Once past these basics, there are several equally desirable extras. Guest accommodations for a sleep-over friend are important and they don't have to be elaborate. Sleeping bags are always popular, and you can ask a young guest to bring one along. The kind made for indoor use are really just zippered comforters and are pretty inexpensive. A trundle bed, cot, air mattress, or deep window seat will all do perfectly well. And if, instead of calling Good Will to pick it up, you move your old fold-out couch into your child's room, you can solve the guest bed problem and provide seating at the same time.

Parental eardrums will appreciate some rudimentary soundproofing, unless you like to hear roller skates on wood floors. Wall-to-wall carpeting does an admirable job; for children's rooms it should be closely woven with dense, but not deep, pile. The long, hairy variety isn't firm enough for many kinds of play and seems to swallow small parts of games and toys. If you can't afford wall-to-wall carpeting, any old area rug will help cut the noise. Some parents choose vinyl flooring for their children's rooms. This should be of the cushioned type with a few small rugs scattered here and there to increase its sound-absorbing capacity. On the ceiling, acoustical tile isn't great to look at but will help reduce the din within. On the walls, cork or burlap bulletin boards are both porous and sound-softening. The main thing to remember: the more soft surfaces—bedspreads, curtains, rugs—the better the room will soak up noise. It's the padded cell effect on a juvenile scale.

A child's room should also include something that's fun to increase its play potential. That something doesn't have to be elaborate; a secret compartment, a peep hole, a ladder, a platform, or a dutch door can all be transformed by a child's imagination. A toy box becomes an ocean liner, an upper bunk a 747. There are jungle gyms designed for children's rooms, but they're on the expensive side. A chinning bar and a trampoline made from a canvas-covered innertube are far cheaper and provide just as much fun. Both can be found in most toy stores and toy catalogues.

FURNITURE FOR KIDS: NOT KIDS' FURNITURE

When furnishing a child's room, the temptation is to buy a whole set of matching youth furniture and then cram it into the area available, regardless of the size of that space. The main drawback to this approach is that furniture geared to juvenile tastes is frequently of inferior quality, both in materials and workmanship, and the designs don't age well. One exception to this is the traditional low table and two small chairs for very young children. They are inexpensive and remain usable for a surprisingly long time.

Rather than laying out a lot of money for that youth ensemble, it usually makes more sense to improvise with pieces of furniture that can be rearranged as needs change. Choose simple styles that are ageless and will grow with the kids. Often, family hand-me-downs, imaginatively painted or papered, work very well. Here are some ideas using pieces you probably already have or that are easy (and inexpensive) to buy.

- A couple of low chests of drawers can be bridged with a wood or Formica top to make a desk, or they can be pushed together to create a storage headboard for a bed. The backs of the chests that form the headboard can be covered with fabric or wallpaper to match the room. If there's an infant in the room, the dressers can be positioned side-by-side and topped with a plastic covered pad to serve as a changing table. This provides a good working surface and storage space, too.
- There is a great variety of stacking plastic drawer modules and bins. Some of the drawers are strong enough to support the same desk-top arrangement as the chests, again giving you flexible storage for anything from crayons and toy cars to clothing.
- Shelving—free-standing or wall-mounted and preferably adjustable—makes an excellent replacement for the traditional bureau. It stores diapers for a baby, toys for a toddler, and books and "collections" for a school-age child.

A bed, though necessary, takes up a great deal of space, so don't overlook the storage possibilities underneath it. One way to break the bed habit is to build a platform or loft. Do-it-yourselfers will find platform or loft beds not all that difficult to build, but all construction must be sturdy and anchored firmly to the bearing member in the wall or supported solidly from below. The floor must also be strong enough to handle the added weight of your handiwork. Remember that any kind of sleeping aerie for kids should have a guard rail for safety.

Given a little imagination, all kinds of above-the-floor accommodations can be constructed and then recycled as time goes on, as long as they have been built to hold standard-size mattresses. The added level frees floor space and is one of the most successful ways there is to divide sleeping from other functions.

Along with the playhouse/bunk pictured in this chapter, another elevated option is a two-level carpeted platform. The higher level should be wide enough to hold a twin mattress plus about ten inches for a safety

Vary the loft bed idea by building one on the "roof" of a playhouse. A twin mattress determines the size of the unit shown here. Embellishments are strictly up to you, but this one features a carport for parking a bike, an interior play space, and decorative wooden shingles for a roof. With the appropriate alterations, presto, it becomes a log cabin or a space station. Rungs, braced between the front panel and the chimney, provide easy access to the bed. A small window cut out in the chimney tower is just for fun. If you feel up to it, install wiring for the front door light. With a bulb of low wattage, it can be the night light, too.

rim. The lower carpeted level can then serve as an open play area, as can any remaining floor space. The two-step platform serves to vary the play area and to separate and elevate the sleeping quarters from the rest of the room. You can build the platforms with removable tops to take advantage of the incredible storage space they create. These bed ideas can easily be adapted to shared rooms.

SHARING A ROOM

Double sleeping accommodations are easier to provide than privacy for two kids who are sharing a room. Privacy becomes more important as children grow up. Thus, the absence of a place to call one's own is typically harder on the older child than on the younger. A room for two should, if possible, allow for some personal space even if it's very limited. Short of dividing the room with a wall, which most of the time isn't practical or possible, the least you can do is create the illusion of privacy with lighting, curtains, shades, shutters, and the like.

Again, flexible and inexpensive is best. A sturdy room-darkening (opaque) window shade to pull down between the beds will block a reading light; a folding screen can do the same thing. An open-shelf divider will define the demarcation line between two children but will not present the barrier a bookcase with a solid back does. A wooden frame, strung with rope and decorated with artwork, hung by clothespins might also do the trick. Bed curtains that pull shut will create a "playhouse" and are very pretty for little girls.

More substantial partitions can be devised, but plan them carefully so they do not block light or air circulation. Ideally, if you're dividing a room permanently, one child should not have to walk through the other's sector to get to her own.

Sometimes it's possible to bisect a room by placing the furniture back to back down the center of the floor, with two sets of matching bookcases, dressers, and desks facing in opposite directions. Some sort of divider should be placed between facing desks, however, so there's a little privacy for homework. Depending on the style of furniture, the pieces also can be alternated back-front-back-front, or one child's desk can face the back of the other's bookcase. Unfinished backs can be covered with mirror to make the space seem larger or with cork to serve as a bulletin board.

Another way to split up a room is with a loft, but you need to have a high ceiling, of about ten feet, to make it worthwhile. Placing the mattresses on the loft frees the rest of the room for study and play. Many lofts are designed with partitions that divide both the space on the loft and the space under it. This assures some privacy for the denizens at all times.

The tried and true method of maximizing floor space in a room shared by two children is to install bunk beds. In the classic version, the beds are stacked one over the other, but many systems are now available that offer L-shapes and other interesting arrangements. Some bunks convert to twin beds; if you choose with an eye to future use, the beds will shed their kiddie associations rapidly.

If you dislike bunk beds and the space permits, you can push two studio couches into an L in a corner. This reduces the amount of floor space the beds use up. In tighter spots you may need to use a trundle bed or high-riser, but one disadvantage is that the second bed is not instantly available for naps or just lounging. There also may be complaints about who sleeps where.

D IS FOR DECORATING

Decorating children's rooms is so intimately connected to providing storage space that it's really impossible to separate the two. Dealing with all the stuff kids amass requires ingenuity. The best strategy is divide and conquer. You might want to look into the following:

- Collect containers of all shapes and sizes that can be lined up neatly on the radiator cover, shoved under the bed, or put in rows on shelves. Baskets, plastic tubs, milk carriers, even colorful or campy cardboard cartons work well for sorting out the junk. For uniformity you can paint them or cover them with Con-Tact paper or leftover wallpaper.
- Decorate a wall with athletic gear in a pleasing pattern or stow it all in a brightly colored plastic garbage can. For wall mounting you can use a pegboard or individual plastic hooks that either stick to the wall or screw into it.
- Use the space under the bed to keep a train set or a road racer out of harm's way. Mount the tracks on fiberboard, smooth side down, so it can slide easily under the bed when not in use.
- Rotate toys. Every few months pack some away, and reintroduce others. There's no child alive who can play with all the toys in her possession at one time, and abandoned toys become interesting again after a vacation.
- Remember that furniture is expensive to replace. Choose classic styles, and let the child's current preoccupations—such as Spiderman and E.T.—be reflected in fabrics and accessories that can be changed from time to time.
- When a boy and a girl share a room, keep the furnishings basic and harmonious—all the same or in the same style but a differ-

ent color. Let each child personalize with accessories—his with, say, Incredible Hulk, or hers with Strawberry Shortcake.

- Children's beds are easier to make when equipped with fitted bottom sheets and a quilted comforter that serves as blanket and bedspread in one. Another approach is to make a cover for a comforter by sewing two single sheets together to form an envelope. (Or you can buy one ready-made—it's called a duvet cover.) Instead of the effort involved in laundering the comforter, you simply remove the cover and throw it into your regular wash.

- For older kids, pillows with washable covers are great for lounging and reading. Younger children love to make boats and islands out of them. All sizes and shapes are possible, with large squares and rolls being particularly popular and versatile.

- A small clothes tree eases the crunch in the closet and encourages a child to hang up his jacket or sweater. A kid's shoe bag can be hooked to one branch of the tree, making it easy for the child to put away his footwear. A row of pegs on a wood strip or any hooks that can be mounted to the wall or inside the closet are also useful for hanging things up.

- Children's closets can be modified. Babies and very young children don't really need closets at all; their clothes can be folded into drawers or stacked on shelves. When hanging space is needed, you might install a low rod and an assortment of hooks on the sides of the closet and on the inside of the door so the child can reach them easily. Add temporary shelving in the empty space above the low rod and use it to store games, toys, linens, or whatever you like. If you choose not to add a low rod, you can put a small dresser or chest in the bottom of the closet that won't interfere with the clothes above. Boys often don't need closets at all. Hang the blazer or Sunday suit on the back of the door, and take over the closet for a laundry, workshop, or study (see Closet Cases in Chapter 10).

TIPS FOR TEENAGERS

Most teenagers need a place to sleep, relax, and study. Although toys have become things of the past, adequate storage space remains crucial because, to make a sweeping generalization, teenagers are messy.

Speaking decoratively, age twelve or thirteen may be the time to move away from the bedroom look. Beds can be transformed into studio couches with slipcovers and contour pillows. On a bed with a headboard and a footboard, roll pillows at both ends will make the bed look more like a couch. Floor pillows are inexpensive and almost essential since

▲

This self-contained unit is actually made from a campaign bed base and two bookshelf units which are readily available at unpainted furniture stores. One bookcase should have a drop-down surface so it can be used as a desk. The canopy frame is, of course, optional, but it is nice for a little girl. The grouping can stand alone in the middle of the room or be pushed against a wall. Centering it around a window will create a particularly nice effect. To prevent shifting, you should bolt the components together. The curved supports for the canopy can be found at many lumberyards.

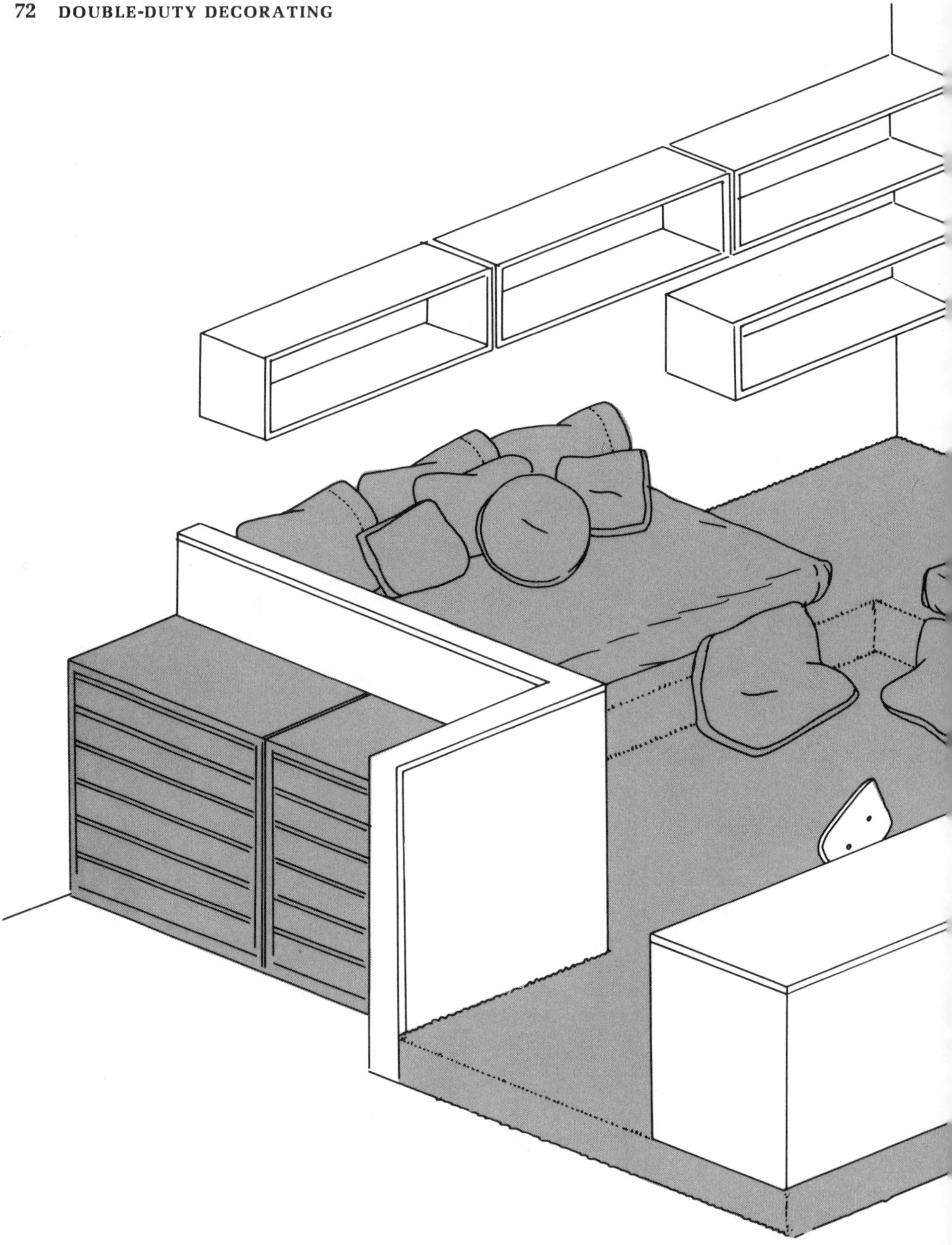

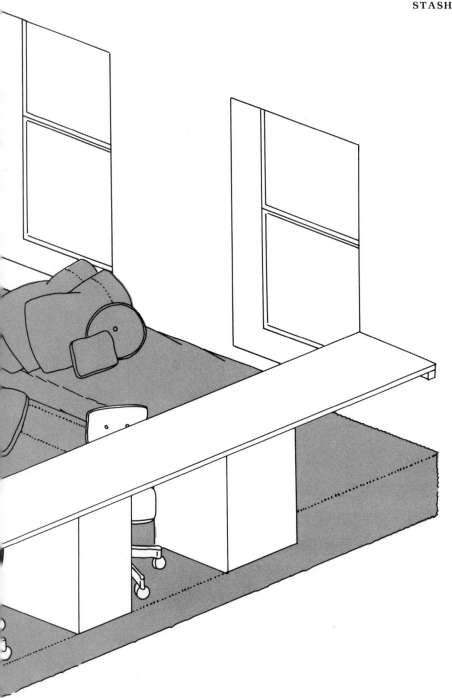

Two teenagers can live together fairly peacefully in a simplified environment like this two-level platform system. Here's how it works. You enter the room just to the left of the pair of dressers that have been lodged in a recess in the lower platform. (Closets are in the wall opposite the window wall and not shown.) The main area consists of an L-shaped platform built on top of the square one. The upper level holds mattresses and pillows; the lower level is for lounging. The double desk is simply a wall-to-wall work surface set on top of storage cabinets. There's plenty of space on the wall above for bulletin boards and open shelving. Carpet the platforms in something durable with a low, dense pile.

teenagers seem to spend so much time on the floor. Three big square pillows will stack into a pile that looks like an ottoman.

For studying, a large sturdy table makes a fine work surface and, if necessary, can be shared by two teenagers. Old partners desks can be found in antique stores or at used office furniture dealers. You can also improvise a double desk with filing cabinets and a deep wood or laminated top. Just face the drawer units in opposite directions.

To keep cleanup under control, the closet should be equipped to handle the teenager's obsession with clothes. Have as many hooks around as you possibly can. A full-size coat rack in the corner of the room can catch the sartorial fallout, which otherwise threatens to obscure every inch of floor space. In addition, some parents opt to supply a large bin to corral garments until they're all dumped unceremoniously into the laundry.

Finally, stereos should be equipped with earphones for private listening—particularly important in a room for two. Furniture purchases should be approached cautiously. Remember: what you buy now will soon be moving into a college dorm or first apartment.

8 WORKING AT HOME

It used to be that only eccentric painters or reclusive novelists worked at home. Not any more. The combination home/office is now the natural habitat of ordinary breadwinners as well. There are advantages to working at home: you can pocket the cost of an office rental, deduct a substantial portion of home expenses from your income tax, or avoid catching the 7:05 A.M. and P.M. But there are disadvantages, too: more noise, less privacy, the intrusion of public on private life and vice versa, lack of space for a proper office, an unprofessional look. Working at home successfully will involve some significant compromises.

A desk alone does not an office make. Most people need some kind of separation—either psychological or physical—of business from home. Witness the distinguished novelist who arises each morning, dresses in a suit and tie, picks up his attaché case, and walks to the other end of the house, where he removes his jacket, loosens his tie, and plunges into his work as if he were a bank executive in a downtown high-rise. The moral of the story: When the commute is across the room instead of across town, some division must be made.

WHERE TO WORK

The challenge in combining an office with another room in the house is creating a suitable businesslike atmosphere without destroying the warm, homey feeling. Clearly there is no one "right" room in which to set up shop, but there are some guidelines to help you decide. First, consider how often and at what time of day the chosen room is used. A bedroom/

▲

   A den, if you are fortunate enough to have one, is a natural site for an office. It's likely there's a desk in there already; all that remains is to make the whole room work together smoothly. Here the room is used as a library as well; when filled, the book-lined walls will be attractive to look at and conducive to cerebral activity. Closed cabinets below the shelves hide files and office supplies. A built-in chest under the window adds more storage space. The couch—the heart of the den—and the table-desk—the core of the office—face the fireplace without facing each other. This gives a unified, yet pleasant, look to the room.

office is fine during the day but less than ideal if you work a great deal at night. In a family with children, there is always too much going on in the kitchen for serious concentration, but a den is an excellent choice—provided the family TV isn't located there. Dining rooms are usually underused and therefore perfect candidates for combination offices. Family rooms are not a good choice because they tend to be messy and they attract noisy crowds after school. Most living rooms can accommodate offices without compromising the decor—which is an important consideration. If you have a house where most of the traffic flows through the back door, you could even convert a foyer, a front hall, or a spacious upstairs landing into an office.

Those who live alone are faced with fewer distractions, but usually they have only one or two rooms in which to incorporate not only an office but sleeping, cooking, and entertaining areas as well. This can be just as frustrating as working in a crowded family household.

FURNISHING YOUR OFFICE

Is the centerpiece of the office going to be an antique Louis XV desk or something that fell off the Bekins moving van? The answer to that question will determine whether the work space will be a decorative plus or a minus. It won't matter if your office is done in drab and dents if you can make it disappear from view, but if you can't hide your desk and files, you'll want them to blend in or even enhance the rest of the decor. If you have a great old desk or a stylish contemporary one, you might well want to show it off.

While an office begins with a desk, it doesn't end there. Good lighting and a comfortable back-supporting desk chair must not be overlooked.

You'll probably also need to make room for all kinds of equipment, among which might be:

telephone	telephone answering machine
typewriter	tape recorder
computer terminal	copier
light box	drawing board
art supplies	file cabinets
ledgers	reference materials

Although much of this stuff is unattractive by nature, finding at least some office equipment that is pleasing to look at isn't as difficult as it used to be. Industrial design has improved enormously; desk chairs are now available with bright-colored upholstery, file cabinets are no longer just gray and can be installed laterally, artist's lights are pretty as well as functional. Since high-tech design has really come into its own, you can choose from a wide assortment of colorful wastebaskets, stackable storage trays, lamps, etc., and make your office a cheerful, contemporary addition to your home.

When new office furnishings are out of the question, some trickery will disguise the obvious shortcomings. Standard file cabinets can be hidden under skirted tables or under a shelf and behind cabinet doors. Covered baskets—sewing baskets, for instance—or large decorative tins are good for concealing desk-top debris. File boxes and accessories can be covered with fabric or marbled paper for a coordinated look. In your bedroom, the typewriter can sport a quilted cover, like a tea cozy, that matches your bedspread fabric.

If you need a typewriter, consider buying a desk designed so that the typing table can be rolled out of sight into a niche. A desk with a sturdy pull-out leaf may be all you'll need if you're using a portable typewriter. An office model, however, is too heavy for such an arrangement, and you'll have to look into buying a sturdy table for it. One factor to take into consideration is that a comfortable typing surface should, ideally, be about three inches lower than normal desk height (30 inches).

LIVING ROOM/OFFICE

An office that is out in the open won't necessarily destroy the charm of your decor, so don't hesitate to look to the living room for a work space. Many living rooms are far too big for just one conversation grouping. By concentrating the social seating at one end—making it more manageable and intimate in the process—you can open the other end for business. An island conversation area, centered in the room, does much the same thing by freeing the periphery. In both cases, the social spaces can be used for informal conferences and meetings.

Lighting should reinforce the division between the two areas. One switch should control the illumination in the office area, and another switch should cover the rest of the room. Thus, a lighted social area can be surrounded by a darkened work space that is invisible at night.

Another approach to separating office space from leisure space is to butt the back of the sofa to the front of the desk. A lamp on the desk can swing back and forth between the two. In a living room, a large table or a flat desk is less obtrusive than other styles of office furniture, but make sure that whatever is on top of the "desk" after the workday is over is more on the order of art than clutter.

DINING ROOM/OFFICE

The dining room, customarily the most underused room in the house, is often an ideal location for an office. With breakfast and lunch bolted

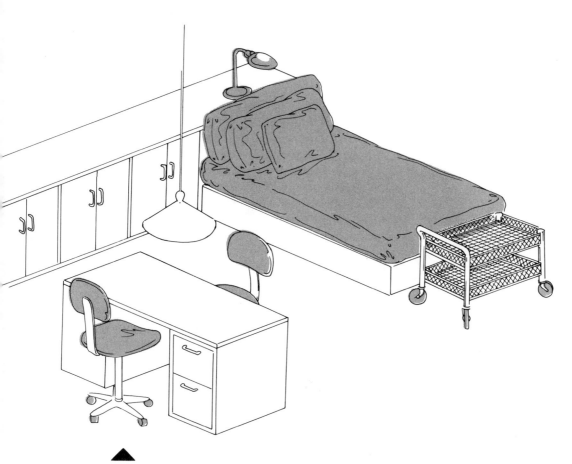

▲

Perhaps most difficult to devise is the room that must be all things—the studio/
apartment/office. This one has been designed to appear custom built when, truth
be told, very little of it needs to be. Low two-door cabinets of any kind—metal
office models, wooden kitchen cabinets, or whatever—look like a single unit
when topped with a long, laminated shelf. The same laminate is used for the bed
platform and desk top. The desk top bridges two file cabinets, facing in opposite
directions, to create a simple double desk. (The depth of the file cabinets determines the width of the top.) Clear of clutter and draped with a tablecloth, the desk
becomes a dining table for two or, without the chairs, a buffet. Other options: add
drawers to the bed's platform base; house a collection of frivolous pillows or an
exotic throw in a big basket to change the mood of the room at the end of the day;
clear the grid cart of papers and files and fill it with food and flowers.

Now you see it, now you don't—the invisible office behind a chic façade of aluminum blinds. This combination sacrifices a minimum of space and leaves the ambience of the dining room intact. But there's more to it than meets the eye. The banquette, a very popular type of dining room seating, can offer storage in its base or be designed to sleep a guest. With the blinds up, the room has the air of a comfortable office/cum conference room; when they're down, there isn't a hint of what goes on behind. The alcove is equipped with wall-mounted shelving. Lighting is provided by a fluorescent tube hidden by a wooden baffle under the bottom shelf. The desk is a pair of classic file cabinets topped with a sheet of plywood. If a great deal of typing is to be done at the desk, the surface for the typewriter should be lowered three inches or the chair should be adjustable to compensate. File cabinets come in various depths, so it's possible to fit this combination into as little as twenty inches.

down in the kitchen or grabbed on the fly, the dining room is empty for sustained periods of time. The dining room table is an ideal conference table or a desk for people who love to spread out. You can clear the table at the end of each day, or if you really don't eat there that often, simply close the door on it, or install an attractive curtain to hide the disarray. If you plan to do a lot of work at the table, the overhead light must be adjustable for comfort; it should pull up and down or be equipped with a dimmer. When adding a desk to the dining room, choose one that complements the style of furniture already there so it can double as a sideboard when you're entertaining. Try to place the office area near a window so it will be more cheerful and less claustrophobic. An armoire or the bottom of a china cabinet is a great place for keeping most office supplies and electrical gadgetry. A wall of credenzas can double as display space or as a sideboard and office storage.

BEDROOM/OFFICE

A bedroom/office will look less like the former and more like the latter if you dispense with most traditional bedroom furniture. Yet to be a success, a bedroom/office must be comfortable and relaxing as well as con-

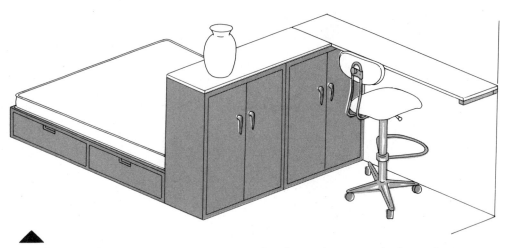

Besides providing storage space, two metal utility cabinets pushed together make a good headboard. Add a shelf along the wall, supported at one end by the cabinets and at the other end by a wall brace, and you have created an L-shaped work area. An artist's chair works well with this arrangement and is both comfortable and adjustable. An alternative approach would be to line up three cabinets along one side of the mattress, which, when topped with large, plump pillows, would look like a low sofa. Leave the cabinets their original high-tech gray or spray paint them to match the bedroom.

▲

Avoiding bedroomy decorating clichés is the first step in designing a room that must serve gracefully as a place to work and a place to sleep. Passing up standard layouts—the bed flanked by twin night tables, the dresser opposite—will also help. Try the bed at an angle or in the center of the room. If the bed must remain against the wall, it should be the same wall in which the door is located; this way the eye falls on the other, "nonbed" features of the room first. The height of the furniture should be more or less uniform. The bed, the low, wall-hugging storage shelves, and the wide work surface pictured here keep things visually harmonious. If the desk area is located next to the bed, they can share the same light source. A single bed looks more like a divan when the headboard and the footboard are identical and used as backrests for pillows. A super-firm mattress, an unupholstered base or a carpeted platform, and tailored covers (instead of dusters or bedspreads) reinforce the room's businesslike tone.

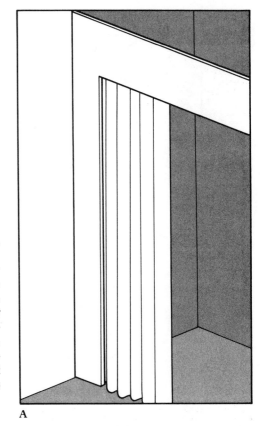

There are several ways to create an alcove. A—Vertical blinds, inset in a partition, can effectively screen off an alcove office. B—A structure such as this one, designed for sewing, can be braced wall to wall and hidden behind pull draperies on traverse rods. C—Hinged screens are a basic but nevertheless adequate way to conceal an office at home. They are flexible and inexpensive to install because they require no carpentry.

A

ducive to work. Your goal is to create a room-within-a-room where, after 5 P.M., your other life begins.

The biggest dilemma of the bedroom/office is that the bed always looks like the bed during the hours when it shouldn't. If you always work alone, nothing need be done, but if clients come to call, it's a disadvantage. The obvious solution is to treat the bed as seating. This is most convincing when the treatment is tailored—fitted cover, comforter, bolsters, and so on. Dividing a double bed into a two-sided sofa with a heavy bolster and assorted pillows down the center is a variation on the wedge-shaped pillow gambit but only works well when the bed is in the center of the room. It may be possible to devise a system where part of the bed slips under something else, perhaps a table you've had specially built, but things like this begin to run into money.

It's important to make the transition from work to leisure something that can be accomplished in minutes. One way to do this is to isolate the bed with bed curtains, so that instead of drawing a curtain across the office, you draw it around yourself. It's like creating your own cocoon. Certainly this is easiest if your bed is a fourposter, but you can also mount

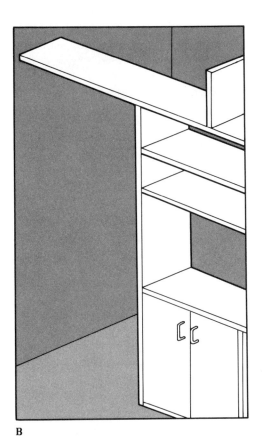

B

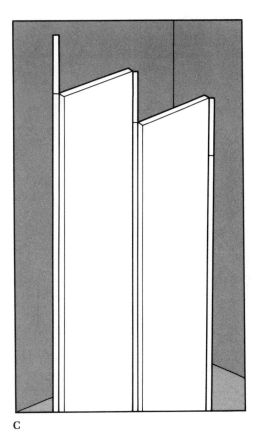

C

hardware on the ceiling and hang the draperies from there. A sleep sofa or a Murphy bed removes the bed from sight but must be reckoned with every morning and evening. Screens and draw draperies also can be manipulated to conceal the bed by day and the office by night.

Insufficient storage means a bed covered in file folders at the end of the day. A bedroom wall unit, built-ins, an armoire, or open shelves equipped with baskets for storing loose items all will help keep the working side of life organized and out of sight when it should be. Under-bed storage is ideal for artwork, blueprints, architectural drawings, and anything else that should be put away flat; the higher the bed, the more you can store underneath.

THE HIDEAWAY OFFICE

For all of us with minds more organized than our desk tops, the disappearing office is a godsend. No one will ever know that things have gone awry with the filing system; you can just shut it away—out of sight, out of mind. The decorative challenge is considerably lessened, too.

Ideal spots for disappearing offices are already present in many houses and apartments or can be added without too much expense. A large closet—particularly one where the long measurement is the width, not the depth—with louvered or bifold doors is easy to adapt for office use. It's not necessary to find a closet large enough to work inside when the door is shut because the closet office simply opens on the room when needed and closes when not.

Lacking a large enough closet or being unable to spare one, you can use an existing alcove and fit the opening with some kind of closure. Failing this, the next choice is to create the alcove. One way is with a divider. The least expensive dividers are also the least substantial, but, depending upon your needs, they may do very well. A system of screens—freestanding or ceiling hung from tracks—shuts off a piece of the room quite successfully, as do draperies, shades, blinds, and folding doors. Consider installing a permanent partition with a large opening or arch that is closed by draperies that either pull or tie back to expose the work area. Besides delineating the space, a permanent partition adds the support needed for shelves and wall-mounted lighting, which screens do not. However, a full partition with a door, instead of an arch, would be claustrophobic. A partition with a large opening actually deducts a very small amount of square footage from a room. A perfectly adequate work area can be laid out in a space only two and a half to three feet deep. (Don't forget to add the thickness of the partition to this figure when making your calculations.) When the office is not in use, it's out of sight, so it's acceptable to be parsimonious about the interior. The divider, however, must look real and substantial. A shaky partition on the verge of collapse will attract the wrong kind of attention and your secret work life won't be secret anymore.

Building closets projecting from each end of a long wall is yet another way to create an alcove (see Chapter 2, "Dividing Lines). Situate the office between the closets, and close it off with mirrored doors or shirred fabric panels. It's not necessary to keep the alcove at right angles to the wall, either. Screening off a corner adds an interesting slant to a room, whether the alcove is delineated by hinged panels or expensive built-in doors.

9 THE GUESTING GAME

Back in the Middle Ages having one guest, or a few dozen, drop in wasn't a problem. Everyone just bedded down by the fire with the dogs. Now, slightly more gracious accommodations are required, but the disappearance of the spare bedroom from many of today's homes means that guests must usually be lodged in busy rooms used primarily for other purposes.

To determine how much space and how many decorating dollars to allot for guest accommodations, figure out how often you are likely to have guests and for how long. A few overnight stays do not demand the facilities or comforts of a week-long visit. Think about who your guests will be, too. Children are more flexible than adults—literally and figuratively; older people may have physical problems that rule out some of the more impromptu sleeping arrangements. Aim for as much comfort for the guest and convenience for the hostess as the budget allows. Some of the easiest and best ideas are the least expensive.

SLEEPING ACCOMMODATIONS

For the occasional guest, a standard, nonconvertible sofa can be made into a bed in minutes, though if under seven feet long it will not be comfortable for some adults. Simply remove the back cushions, if any, and protect the upholstery with a mattress pad before tucking in the sheets. An average sofa can hold one adult or two small children sleeping with their heads in opposite directions. However, be careful not to use a sofa as a bed too often because the springs will be damaged.

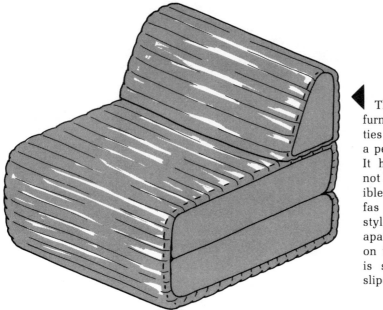

This type of foam-slab furniture unsnaps or unties and then unfolds into a perfectly adequate bed. It has the advantage of not looking like a convertible. Chairs sleep one, sofas sleep two. Beware of styles that shift or slide apart when you're sitting on them—a problem that is sometimes solved by slipcovering.

Traditional convertible sofas and chairs are the modus operandi in numerous homes without guest rooms. In some styles, a hidden mattress folds out of the base; in others, individual components are rearranged to make a bed; still others fold out to form a mattress when straps or mechanisms are released. Convertible sofas range in size from single to king, but before choosing the most grandiose, remember to allow sufficient space for the opened bed as well as room to walk around it comfortably. And remember that when sleeping and sitting surfaces are one and the same, the bed will have to be made up every time it is used.

A high-riser conceals a second bed under what appears to be a studio couch. The second bed, which pulls out on casters, can be kept made up and ready for guests. Decoratively, high-risers are something of a liability because they always look like exactly what they are, and they're too high to afford sofa-style seating, even when fitted with bolsters or cushions, although a double rank of pillows will help.

A studio couch is really more of a bed than a couch and ideally should not be placed in a room where it will be used primarily for seating. A tailored slipcover and contour cushions will make it look less like a bed, and seating comfort will improve if the mattress is firm.

The rollaway bed—a folding mattress and springs on casters—must be kept in a closet. It opens into adequate sleeping accommodations for one but is bulky to store and unwieldy to move up and down stairs. Camp cots are compact and take up less room than a rollaway, but they leave a lot to be desired as far as comfort goes unless they're topped with some

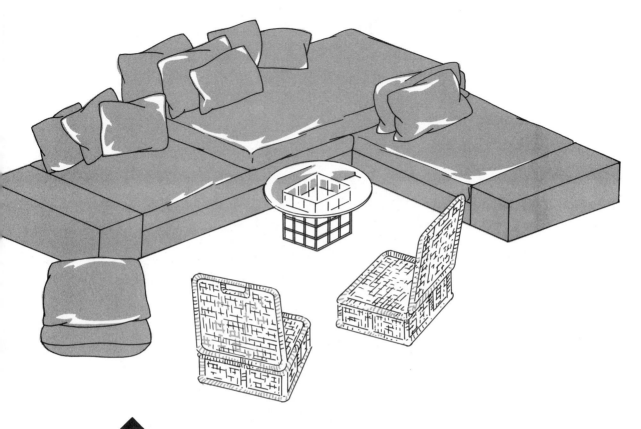

This platform sofa is a relatively uncomplicated do-it-yourself project consisting of an L-shaped platform of plywood, covered with straw matting you attach with a staple gun. On top are three twin mattresses upholstered in a sturdy cotton ticking. When guest accommodations are needed, the top mattress is simply pulled off and the two remaining ones are made up with contour sheets. The straw beach chairs sitting opposite the sofa have handy storage space for linens in their bases.

kind of mattress. Light easy-to-assemble models are available from army/navy stores and hunting/camping outfitters.

An air mattress, with a sleeping bag or fluffy comforter, makes quite a respectable bed if the guest doesn't mind sleeping on the floor. Everything required, including the pump to inflate the mattress, can be kept in a small chest that doubles as a table.

Futons, the Japanese answer to sleeping on the floor, are thick pads that fold for storage by day but are deliciously comfortable to sleep on at night. They also can fold against the wall to form chairs and sofas. Futons are as attractive to look at as they are to sleep on. Paired with a thick comforter, they are the best of the store-away solutions to the guest accommodations problem.

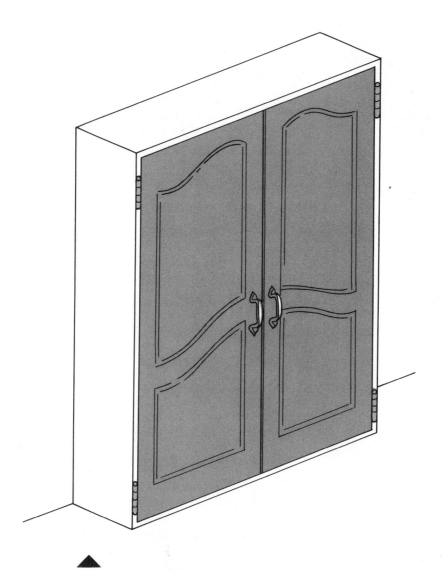

Open a Murphy bed and out fall the Marx Brothers—at least that's the public's image of these beds that fold up into a wall or a cabinet. But housing guests is no laughing matter. Here both the Murphy and the mechanism that raises and lowers it are enclosed in a doored cabinet. Often the cabinet is equipped with bedside lights and shelving. A Murphy bed takes up about the same amount of space as a standard wall unit. Manufacturers sell Murphy bed wall systems with storage and desk units to match. Unfortunately, many of these are just plain ugly or of pedestrian design. It's often cheaper, and certainly more original, to purchase the mechanism and have the cabinet built to order. A pair of doors scavenged from an armoire or unearthed at a furniture wreckers give a Murphy bed the look of a Eu-

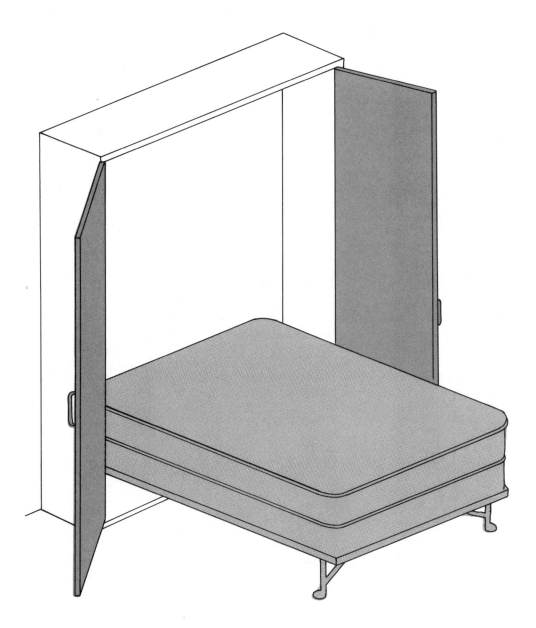

ropean "placard." Plain wood doors covered in mirror also are very attractive. Murphy beds can be installed along a wall or across a corner. The latter creates an interesting angle, but sacrifices a bit of space. Single beds fold horizontally as well as vertically. Keep in mind that any furniture in front of the doors should be light enough to be moved easily.

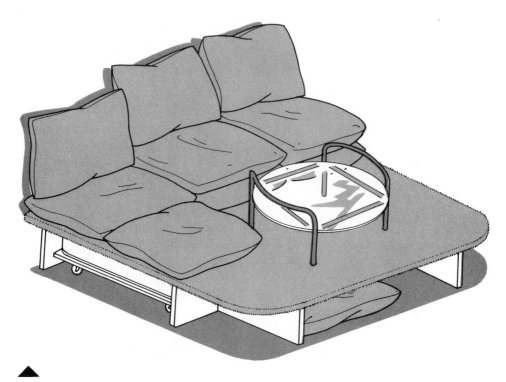

▲

An open-sided, carpeted platform, less than a foot off the floor, can house a plywood base bed on casters with a foam mattress on top. The bed rolls under the platform into its own compartment. Bedding may also be stowed underneath. For the top of a small platform, unstructured pillow furniture is a good choice; a larger one could carry off more substantial footed pieces. Note: This illustration is drawn so you can see what's going on. In real life the lip of the platform, as well as the fact that it is so near the floor, would make the underpinnings much less obtrusive.

YOUNG GUESTS

If a trundle or bunk bed is part of a child's room, one child can move into another's, freeing an entire room for guests. A trundle under the parents' bed allows a child to move in temporarily when he is displaced by a visitor.

A young infant can be made at home in a dresser drawer (the bottom one, left open of course), in a laundry basket, or even in a cardboard carton—an egg pullman is perfect. An old cradle storing firewood by the hearth or filled with a collection of antique dolls can revert to its original purpose when a very small visitor arrives. A toddler can be bedded down in two upholstered armchairs pushed together (tie the legs together if they tend to pull apart). The arms act as sides so he won't fall out.

If you're short of storage space and also need a spot to sleep a guest, the problem is easily solved by building a pair of closets with a wide window seat in between. The window seat base pictured here opens for storage. The mattress (about equal to a standard twin mattress) is made of three thick cushions rather than one, so getting at what's underneath doesn't take much effort. The ideal location for this seat/bed/storage area is a wall with windows in the center. An arrangement like this will sleep one adult or two children with their heads at opposite ends.

TIPS ON COMFORT

For comfort and privacy, locate guests in the least trafficked areas of the house. Dining rooms and studies are particularly good candidates. Even if you have a genuine guest room, it makes sense to combine it with another function, such as a sewing room or a dressing room. Just make sure it's doing *something* to earn its keep and energy costs.

Regardless of whether guests have a room of their own or are camping out in the middle of the den, a few little extras will make their stay more pleasant. Make sure the bedside light can be turned off without getting out of bed so a guest does not have to stumble around unknown territory in the dark. Provide a folding screen for privacy. It also will help keep out morning light if the room cannot be darkened with shades or blinds. Offer a sleeping mask. Clear a few hangers in the closet and a flat surface on a desk, dresser, or table for a suitcase. Folding suitcase racks are inexpensive and can be purchased from many mail-order catalogues. A portable standing towel rack allows the guest to separate his towels from the usual jam-up in the bathroom. All the other items of hospitality—toothbrush, scented soap, reading material, cologne, crackers, and hard candy—can be presented prettily in a bedside basket.

10 NOOKS AND CRANNIES

The fact that you can shut a closet is both a blessing and a bane. Close the door and mismatched overshoes, old Girl Scout uniforms, and the 1972 Peoria telephone directory are rendered invisible. You can't see them, but they're there, just like the Loch Ness monster. Unfortunately, closets themselves often cause the closet problem. Many are too small, too high, too narrow, or too deep. They encourage a "throw it in and shut the door" mentality. A house or apartment already too snug for comfort can't afford the extra poundage of cast-off, outgrown, or broken items.

The first step in tackling the closet problem is to ask yourself, "What's in there that I really use?" Clearing out a closet maximizes its storage capabilities and frees up valuable space. Newly liberated closets can be turned to other, better uses and can even function as miniature rooms.

WORKING WITH WHAT YOU'VE GOT

Most closets come equipped with only one hanging bar and a single shelf, hardly the latest in closet design and a waste of storage possibilities. Older houses seem to have the most idiosyncratic closets. Combining two of them, if they're adjacent, will frequently more than double the usable space. New houses offer bigger closets, but because the space is not always well laid out, they hold little more than the tiny, old-fashioned kind. The wide closet with louvered folding doors that is typically found in new houses and apartments is the perfect candidate for a makeover. Half of it can usually do the entire job the closet was intended to do, leaving the other half available for intriguing new uses.

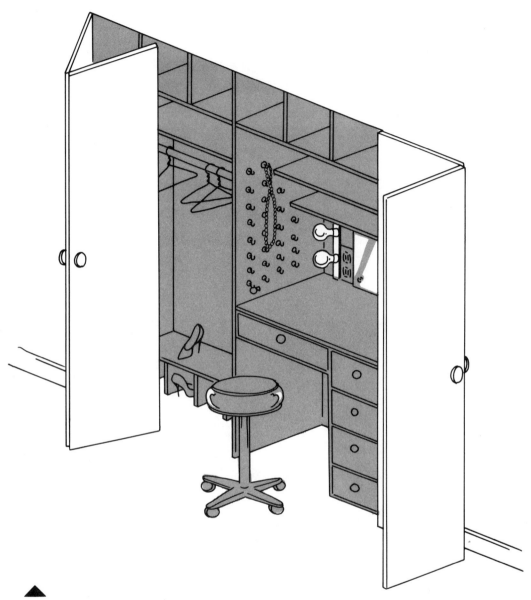

Half, or less, of a standard clothes closet—the kind with fold-back doors—can be converted into a dressing table/vanity area. Sometimes a dressing table can be moved directly into the closet. If not, a shelf that is attached to one side of the closet and rests on a small chest (or any storage unit) will do as well. Mirror, glass, or laminate make good surfaces for a dressing table top. Give an old stool a shirred skirt and tuck it underneath the dressing table when not in use. A stool on casters is also handy. Sort all beauty aids into simple compartments to eliminate the usual jumble: all nail care items together; all skin creams together; perfume, makeup, and hair care potions in separate baskets or labeled plastic tubs to pull out as needed. Install an electric outlet for the blow-dryer and/or hot rollers.

Closet renovations can be as simple as installing more hanging bars, shelves, dividers, racks, and drawers and as logical as consolidating all sewing, sports, or audio paraphernalia in one place. Some closet transformations require ripping out and rebuilding; others can be done without severely altering the existing space. There are designers who specialize in redoing closets. You should consult one if your job is particularly complex.

The location of a closet can limit the metamorphosis that it may undergo. Better not turn a closet into a lavatory if it's situated off the living room because privacy would be less than ideal. If you want a telephone booth, it should be in a quiet place not adjacent to the den, where the television could interfere with normal conversation, unless you can soundproof the area adequately. Moving one's laundry to an upstairs closet close to bedrooms and hampers is a great idea, but the new site must be within reasonable distance of water and, perhaps, gas lines or the price tag on the move will be exorbitant.

IF YOU DON'T HAVE ONE . . . BUILD ONE

All of this assumes that houses and apartments come equipped with enough closets to begin with, which is almost never the case. When the number of closets is hopelessly inadequate, building more is the next step. Closet construction is generally not complicated or difficult, but finding the right location may be. An experienced carpenter will be able to advise you on the where's and how's of your particular situation.

A long narrow room can be fitted with closets by building a pair at one end, one on either side of the window. This creates an alcove or window seat while it brings the length of the room into better proportion. A wide room may be narrowed by building a series of closets and cupboards that extends the full length of one wall.

Unused square footage on landings can be converted into a closet, as can the space under the stairs, or fit doors across the area under the eaves, and install lots of shelves. A triangular closet, although not always good for items that must be hung, can hold boxes, trunks, and what have you.

An armoire, the "closet" when houses didn't come equipped with closets, is the most decorative solution to storage space shortages. These antiques become increasingly valuable with the passing years, and the interiors can be arranged to hold clothes, electronics, china, practically anything. The trick is to organize the space inside so not one precious inch is wasted. Modern wall units can serve the same function but rarely with the same touch of class.

A desk in a closet sounds claustrophobic but isn't when the door is removed. Remove the door moldings, too, for a more finished look. Since this setup is always on view, the components should be chosen with care. If the closet is located in the kitchen, install matching kitchen cabinets against the back wall or repaint or wallpaper old cabinets. The work surface can be made of any durable material and it should fill the entire area. A center drawer, such as the one shown here which matches the cabinetry, would be a nice extra. Lighting can be provided by fixtures mounted underneath the cabinets. Add a phone for convenience as well as stick-on cork squares to pin up the calendar, and the car-pool schedule. When a child needs a quiet place for doing homework this could be the spot. Keep all correspondence here, all bills and appliance warranties. A home office like this helps keep personal and family business papers organized and separate from those that pertain to other work.

It's the fate of the home sewer to wander from room to room like a nomadic "Coco" Chanel; cut it out in the dining room, sew it in the bedroom, fit it in front of the hall mirror. For a serious seamstress a centralized location is a must, but if you don't have the luxury of a room devoted to sewing, a closet is the next best thing. Any closet not in the middle of a traffic pattern will do. It's not necessary to invest in anything fancy here—strictly functional is your best bet. If your sewing machine isn't built into a console, a metal utility table sold in houseware stores or an old typing table makes a most acceptable surface. If the closet isn't wide enough to sew in comfortably, the table should be on casters so it can roll in and out. Upper shelves can hold fabrics, patterns, sewing baskets, button boxes, and other necessities. The baffle (shown here on the lowest shelf) conceals a lighting fixture. Baskets hold notions, yarn, knitting needles, scissors, and name tags. Store spools on rows of nails or a thread holder mounted inside the door. Hang a full length mirror on the outside. A laundry basket under the table (instead of the stool pictured here) can catch the mending as it piles up.

A laundry closet is a boon to apartment dwellers and to homeowners without basements. To keep installation costs in line, choose a closet that backs up to a bathroom or kitchen so the water and waste lines can be easily tapped. A gas dryer may involve moving or extending a gas line, which can be expensive. An electric dryer, which requires 220-volt current, may mean installing special wiring, also no cheap undertaking. Make sure the closet is wide enough to get the machines in without ripping out the frame, and that there is enough breathing space around them. If stackables don't fit because they're excessively tall, Whirlpool and Frigidaire manufacture all-in-one washer/dryers that go half as high. If the stackables are too wide, Hoover and others make minimachines that will fit in all but the narrowest closets. Side-by-side models need considerably more room but can be installed in a wide closet with folding doors. Depending on the space available, the closet can accommodate a laundry basket and some linen storage. Use the inside of the door to hang the ironing board, detergent, and other supplies, but make sure there's sufficient clearance for the door to shut once the caddies are in place.

Plant lovers usually keep their pots and potting soils under the sink, while the rest of their gear is scattered from garret to garage. An indoor gardener's closet puts it all behind one closed door. Light upper shelves with neon tubes and use them for a plant nursery. If the shelves are wire grid, the same neon tubes will illuminate the entire closet. Other shelves can hold cachepots, vases, baskets, dried moss, and other supplies. A small plastic trash can will keep a budding Luther Burbank in potting soil for at least a year. Fill another can with vermiculite. Leave the main work area open, and hang the tools of the trade—shears, florist's tape, wire, knives—from hooks on a pegboard. A small sink and running water would be helpful but aren't absolutely necessary and may be costly to install if the nearest plumbing is too far away. A dustpan and brush or a small electric sweeper is a must because gardening is messy. A minirefrigerator is a real luxury, but makes forcing bulbs a snap. (You can bring in electricity from any nearby ceiling fixture, wall plug, or switch.) Use the inside of the closet door for hanging work clothes and gardening gloves.

Whether you decide to make do with an existing closet or build one from scratch, here are a few tips on how you can use it rather than just store a jumble of unrelated objects.

- *Hobby closet.* Keep all the stamps, butterflies, needlework, rock collections, and their related bits and pieces in one place. Install a shelf or small desk as well as attractive plastic storage units in a renovated closet, and you can have all your hobby tools right at your fingertips.
- *Audio closet.* Amplifier, stereo, turntable, tape deck (and all their unsightly wires), tapes, and records stay out of the living room—or at least out of sight—in a closet with adjustable shelving.
- *Cedar closet.* Here's an easy, inexpensive do-it-yourself project. Line a closet with cedar planks from the lumberyard, and add hanging bars and shelves for box storage. Cedar protects woolens from hungry insects. Every few years sand the planks to bring back the scent.
- *Auxiliary pantry.* A closet adjacent to a kitchen can take a lot of the burden off cramped cabinets and shelves. Fit the closet with narrow shelves for canned goods; leave room for storing bulky paper goods above and heavy containers of oil or other very large cans below. Inside the door, mount top-to-bottom wire racks to hold spices, condiments, and other small cans and bottles.
- *Telephone booth.* Transform an idle closet into a phone booth for teenagers who want privacy and for their parents who would like to reclaim their phone. Include a ventilation fan and a doodling surface, and put a carpet remnant and throw pillows on the floor.
- *Powder room.* Everyone needs more washroom space, so squeeze an extra toilet and handwashing facilities into a closet with the help of minisinks and compact fixtures designed to fit into tight corners. But keep in mind the cost of installing the necessary plumbing if it isn't already at hand.
- *Sauna.* Saunas are available from several manufacturers and are ready to be installed in almost any closet. Saunas are relaxing as well as therapeutic, and one will glamorize even the most humdrum apartment.
- *Summer/winter clothes closet.* In a high-ceilinged closet, replace out-of-reach shelves with a hanging rod for out-of-season clothes. Add hooks for belts and purses and shelves for boxes of shoes.
- *China closet.* Fit a closet that's near the dining room with shelves. Use the top section for trays in slots, the punch bowl,

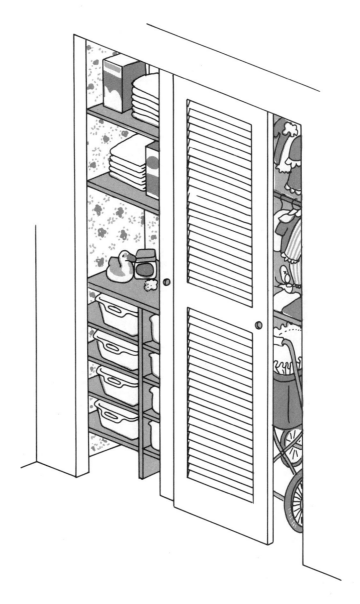

▲

   While babies come in small packages, their equipment does not. A closet in the nursery is an ideal baby care center—clothes, toys, diapers, bedding, and bathing supplies in one place. Given proper ventilation, you can even put infant sleeping accommodations in a closet, but babies outgrow the space too quickly to make it worthwhile for anything but the most temporary use. A simple storage center, however, can be rearranged as the child grows up. A strong, padded shelf is the main feature; it eliminates the need for a changing table in the baby's room. Clothes are sorted into individual plastic dish tubs stored on shelves. Other shelves hold diapers, toiletries, and medicines safely out of the way. If the closet is wide enough to partition, one side can be fitted out with expansion hanging rods to be moved apart as needed.

and large serving pieces. Save the center for silver and china. Construct wide closely spaced shelves on the bottom for linens and mats.

- *Wine cellar.* Line the walls of a closet in the basement or near the kitchen with floor-to-ceiling bottle storage. Floor bins are useful for jug wines. If price is no object, you might want to investigate custom-built closet wine cellars that come with climate controls and other expensive options.
- *Workshop.* Create a well-equipped workshop for the weekend carpenter. Consolidate all tools and materials in a closet fitted with a pegboard and various storage compartments. A work surface can be built with space underneath to store a folding workbench with clamps and vises attached to it.

Under the Stairs

"Thou shalt not waste the space underneath the stairs" should be a commandment for those in need of elbow room. The space under the typical one-story flight of steps—the type without jogs or turns and without another stairway descending directly below it—can be turned to a remarkable number of uses. Sometimes, depending on the manner of construction, this triangular space has been left open, and sometimes a panel covers the space to make the stairway appear solid all the way to the floor. When the staircase has such a soffit, you have to cut into it to get at the space behind, and after you've done so, you'll have to work around the supports. If you try to change the arrangement of supports under the

◀ *Opposite:* A home bar makes entertaining easier, but most of the freestanding varieties look terrible. A bar in a closet looks more substantial and doesn't intrude on the rest of the decor. It also disappears entirely when you close the door. Locate the bar closet in the front hall or in a former coat closet. If the living room is the preferred location, but the nearest closet opens on the hall, simply seal up the hall closet opening and break through into the living room. Still no closet? Build a pair—creating an alcove in the process. Put the bar in one and use the other for party-giving equipment. The perfect bar closet has a small refrigerator and a sink as well as storage for glassware, liquor, and wine. Houseware departments sell an amazing variety of racks and holders designed to facilitate stemware storage. You must have a work surface to mix drinks on and it's a good idea to have drawers to hide the openers, stirrers, shakers, and so on. Some decorating tips: make the counter-top out of tile, butcher block, marble, or laminate plastic; mirror the backsplash; polyurethane wine labels to the wall to make impromptu wallpaper; install a length of brass foot rail. Note: If the light source is from above, glass shelves will allow it to come through better.

stairs, remember they serve a crucial structural function (holding up the steps) and should *not* be modified without obtaining expert guidance. You'll also find that staircases with closed risers offer more possibilities than those with open ones.

STICK IT UNDER THE STAIRS

One of the easiest and least expensive under-the-stairs options is to redesign the space for storage. You can transform it into a clothes closet, either with hanging rods or with pull-out bins on casters. Both methods offer a convenient way to store your summer things in winter or your winter things in summer. Folding doors close it from view. You can also use the space to solve some of your thornier storage problems, such as where to put the extra leaves for the dining room table, or the artificial Christmas tree, or your snow tires. Another possibility is to make the space into a broom closet for the various vacuum cleaners, floor polishers, mops, buckets, and cleaning supplies that have never had a home big enough to accommodate them.

When a stairway is located near the kitchen, the underside is ideal for use as a pantry. It can also store all the kitchen supplies you need only once in a while—the fondue pot, the 25-cup coffee percolator, the blender. Party supplies, such as the folding table and chairs, the ice bucket, cocktail napkins, and colored toothpicks, are all easily accessible and quickly out of the way stored beneath the stairs.

UMPTEEN OPTIONS

When a stairway descends into a hall, the deft use of the space underneath greatly expands the usefulness of the hall itself. By installing a playhouse or a toy closet under the stairs, the hall functions as a play room, a handy circumstance if your home lacks a suitable play area.

Think of building a wine cabinet under stairs that come down in a cellar. With this arrangement you can have cool wine whenever you need it and have it stored properly and conveniently out of the way. If you're really organized, you should be able to pick out just the right bottle when your guests arrive.

Fit the underside of stairs that adjoin a family room or a living room with attractive shelving. In effect, this gives you a custom-made wall unit where you can store the television and related video equipment, the stereo and records, and books. You could also turn this triangular space into a cocktail cabinet for storing liquor and cocktail gadgetry. Confirmed collectors could fill the shelves with their treasures. Indirect lighting would make this arrangement even more pleasing and would add very little to

A compact home office fits neatly under the stairs, and, if the adjacent wall is incorporated, you can end up with a fairly spacious L-shaped work surface as well. The work surface can be wall-mounted, supported by drawer units, or a combination of the two. Covering the wall with pegboard is a practical and inexpensive way to organize office supplies. You might hang up one of those molded plastic storage units with individual compartments for pencils, tape, paper clips, etc. If your under-the-stairs office seems a mite claustrophobic, you can lessen the feeling by mirroring one wall. For illumination, a wall-mounted desk lamp on a flexible arm works best, but don't forget to install the electric outlet before you put in the desk. Leave a space underneath the desk for a trash can, and be sure to position the knee-hole in such a way that you don't bump your head on the stairs above.

the cost. If you need more space for seating you could create a built-in cushion-covered bench. If you make it with a removable seat cover, you can use the bottom for storage.

Much of what you can do with closets can also be done with the space under the stairs. You can practically make it into another room. A home workshop or a sewing center is a good candidate for this space. If you're willing to invest the money in rewiring or rerouting pipes, you could turn under-the-stairs-space into housing for a washer and dryer, a half-bath, or a telephone booth.

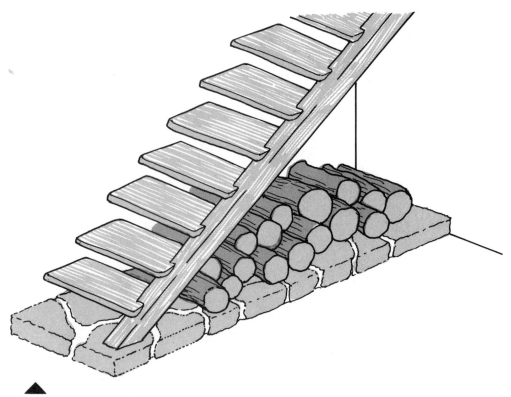

▲

A staircase with open risers offers limited possibilities for storage, but it does make a perfect spot for stacking a winter's worth of firewood. You also might consider filling the area with a row of oversized lidded baskets or large earthenware urns. You can keep toys, sewing fabrics, or anything you wish, inside them. A blanket chest will slip into the space nicely if your taste runs to American country decor.

The space under the stairs makes an ideal location for a playhouse—with or without a door to shut it off. Should you choose to have one, a Dutch door would be more fun for children than a standard door. By painting the exterior with clouds and a tree, a smoking chimney or a turret, you'll help your child's imagination along. Use the playhouse to shelter your collection of rolling stock—tricycles, wagons, and the like—when it's not being used by the youngsters.

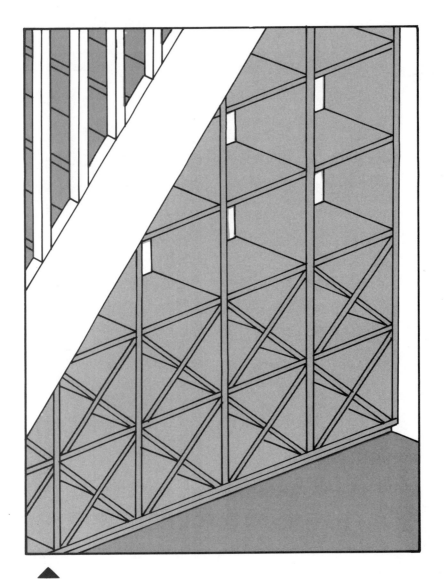

▲

If there's simply not enough storage room in the kitchen, the space under the basement or back stairs will greatly expand it. Broken into compartments, this area can hold canned goods, oversized casseroles, stock pots, and other bulky items that you need frequently but which take up a large amount of space. A wine connoisseur might create a wine cellar under the basement stairs (especially if it's an excavated basement), an ideal spot for wine storage because the temperature remains on the cool side all year round. If wine is stored in the main part of the house, you might add iron-grille or louvered doors to the front of the storage area for a decorative and practical finishing touch. Closing in the wine rack will help ensure that the bottles are not subjected to extremes of temperature or light. One last caution about storage under basement stairs: To make maximum use of the space, you may have to dehumidify a damp basement or waterproof one that leaks.

A cozy place to relax and a spare bed can be one and the same under the stairs. You might choose to fit a mattress covered in sturdy fabric into the space and add pillows covered in the same or contrasting fabric for a backrest. A more elaborate treatment might consist of a built-in plywood base with pillows and mattress equipped with zippered slipcovers. If space permits, the platform base could include a level area that functions as a table (pictured here). The base could also have a hinged lid for storage. Add a pin-up lamp to provide just the right amount of light, if you like.

11 SHELF LIFE

A shelf certainly isn't the most exciting or revolutionary decorating idea going, but it's also not tricky or expensive. With a bit of imagination, a shelf in the right spot is worth any number of fancier alternatives.

A shelf can stand in for furniture you can't afford right now or substitute for something you may need for only a limited time. Among other things, a shelf can masquerade as a desk, dressing table, sideboard, bedside table, or china cupboard. It takes only the right accessories to begin the transformation. Putting up a shelf is certainly more practical and inexpensive than investing in a piece of furniture for a house or an apartment where you're living only temporarily, and sometimes a shelf is all you need to make a room go double-duty.

A shelf in an unusual shape or of eye-catching material stands in for a missing focal point when whatever you put on it—an antique clock, a vase full of silk flowers, a samovar—is worthy of attention. Shelves can go around corners, bridge an alcove and the space between radiators, or connect two juts in a wall. A narrow shelf, running around the periphery of a room a few inches below the ceiling, fills in for the crown molding the builder didn't bother to install and can show off a collection of plates, figurines, or baskets to great advantage. In a room with a long, uninterrupted wall, consider building a table-height shelf the length of the wall. The space underneath the shelf will be divided naturally by the supports, while the top could be used for sewing, hobbies, and writing or as a display area for ornaments or pictures.

Even when your goal is mostly to gain storage space, a shelf should be more than another catchall for junk. A shelf *is* what's on it. You have to look at it, so join the fight against creeping packs of breath mints, old ticket stubs, spare car keys, and unpaid bills that turn the sightly unsightly in less time than it takes to empty your coat pockets.

Take advantage of a small foyer or create the illusion of an entryway with this shelf that does a good imitation of a Victorian hall butler. The more decorative the shelf the better; this goes for the brackets, too. Under the shelf there's a chest for boots, outdoor shoes, or skates. Above the shelf, there's an old mirror for last minute primping. A milk can, painted to look like old tole, holds umbrellas, while wall-mounted hooks hold hats, coats, and keys.

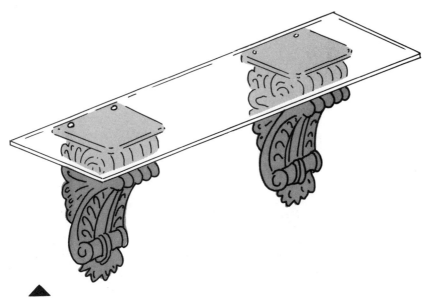

Check out antique stores, junk shops, and the wreckers for interesting supports to rest a shelf on. If you come up empty handed, it's possible to buy plaster reproductions of building ornaments as well as decorative wood supports from hardware stores and mail-order building specialty houses. Use a pair to create a long shelf that might make a good buffet or a single one as a pedestal to hold a very special treasure worthy of spot lighting. If you want a glass shelf, make sure it's thick enough to bear the load you have in mind without bowing.

WHAT MAKES A SHELF

There are as many materials to make shelves from as there are uses for them once you've put them up. If your choice is wood, you can paint, stain, oil, wax, or shellac it. You can also give it a lovely antique look by painting it white and then rubbing off most but not all of the paint with a rag before coating the shelf with polyurethane. Other interesting finishes are *faux bois* and *faux marble,* surfaces that imitate the distinctive grain

There's more than one way to build a shelf, and while this one is more complicated than most, it adds a touch of visual interest as well as storage space. In your dining room/living room, this hollow, triangular prism shelf is deep enough to hold dessert plates, cocktail napkins, playing cards, and serving dishes. They all disappear behind sliding doors. With stools stowed underneath, the ledge becomes a roosting spot—ideal for guests during a buffet dinner. You could have a shelf like this made to order and finish it yourself to cut costs.

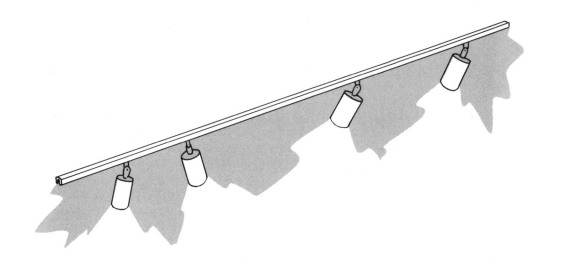

▲

A laminated shelf can serve as a buffet in a dining area where you don't have space for a traditional one and as a resting place for packages and mail the rest of the time. With fluorescent lighting installed behind the bottom front lip, the shelf can be a pleasant source of indirect light and a basket of greenery would thrive underneath. The unit can be fastened to the studs with screws and plugs or with molly bolts in hollow walls. You also may need to brace the shelf underneath with angle irons.

Making room for a family picture gallery in the dining room, foyer, or hallway is yet another trick a well-placed shelf can pull off. The one constant about family pictures is that you're always taking more of them, so instead of making holes in the wall, increase your flexibility with the idea shown here. A narrow shelf with a small lip allows a row of framed photos to lean against the wall. You can switch them around—and add and subtract—at will.

of wood and the look of marble but are painted on. Of course, you can find wallpaper or Con-Tact paper that looks like wood or marble to cover the shelf, but the results won't be nearly as elegant. Don't overlook the real thing either—a beautifully grained or veneered wooden shelf or a slab of marble. Formica makes ideal shelves because it is practically impervious to damage; glass is more fragile but gives a room an airier feeling. Scavengers can recycle the top of an old chest or half a table top; just make sure it's not a rare antique before getting out the saw.

Until you can afford the antique cupboard you've been looking for, this simple arrangement of triangular shelves will do. The shelves rest on cleats and fit snugly into the corner. If the shelves are grooved, it's easy to lean plates against the wall because the groove keeps the bottom rims of the dishes securely in place. You can also use thumbtacks or small nails to keep the plates in line. Two "cupboards" like this in adjacent corners will give any dining room a delightful country look, and one alone will help supply ambiance to the dining end of a combination living room/dining room. If you wish to store everyday dishes on your cupboard, install cup hooks under one of the shelves to avoid stacking cups precariously.

PUTTING IT UP

How you put up a shelf depends on a variety of things, most notably what your walls are made of. Some walls are solid—concrete, brick, stone, concrete block, and brick covered with plaster. These are usually the outside or bearing walls that actually hold up or are part of the building structure. If you want to attach something directly to one of these, you should use long masonry nails or, as is more commonly done, drill holes with a masonry bit and then fit them with a plug and a screw.

Some walls are made of wallboard attached to wooden studs. When this is the case, it is best to locate the studs by tapping on the wall. The wallboard will sound hollow where there's no stud and will give off a dull thump if you hit where there's a structural member. Nail or screw to these wood supports. If a wall is made of wallboard without any reinforcing studs, you must use special toggle or butterfly bolts that open up on the other side of the wallboard to spread the load.

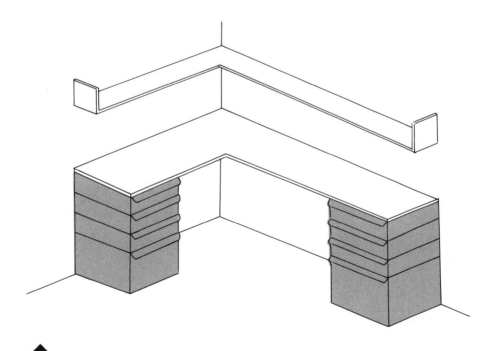

▲

An L-shaped shelf, supported by stackable drawer units and attached to the wall with angle irons, is an easy, do-it-yourself way to provide your child with an inexpensive desk. Another shelf, directly above, can hold school books, a dictionary, and other supplies. The setup is ideal for a basement or family room, too.

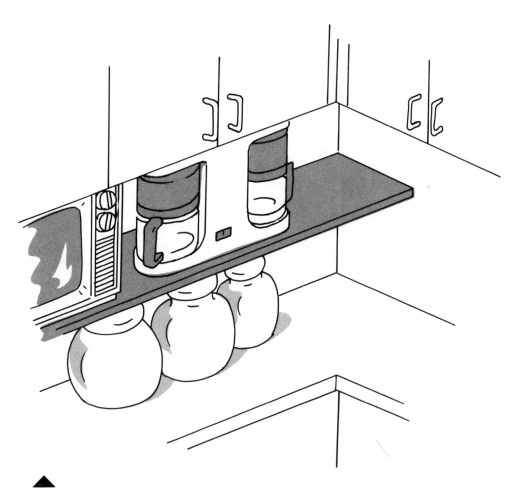

Apartment kitchens are generally unsatisfactory. One common shortcoming is that the cabinets are installed so high you can't reach anything, and a large amount of wall space between the cabinets and the counter is wasted. That's the spot you're looking for. Add a sturdy shelf to hold some of your most frequently used appliances or even a TV, and you've cleared counter space for food preparation.

Another method is to attach a cleat, or strip of wood, to the wall and then hang a shelf from it. The cleat can also be used to support a shelf from underneath in a corner or recess. Of course, the cleat must be nailed or screwed into the studs of a wallboard wall, or attached with masonry nails or screws and plugs to a solid wall. If you are having glass or Plexiglas shelves made, ask the supplier about correct installation procedures.

Hardware stores sell all kinds of decorative brackets, vertical supports, angle irons, and so on that you can use to mount a shelf on the wall. Shop

▲
The luxury of a dressing table is yours for the price of a piece of plywood, dressed up to look like a vanity table. Suddenly you've created a boudoir for yourself, whether you choose to tuck it into a bathroom or make it part of the master bedroom. Mount the plywood on the wall with brackets—it's not important what they look like since they won't be seen—and have a mirror or a piece of glass cut the same size as the shelf for a pretty, spillproof surface. Then attach a gathered skirt to the plywood with Velcro tape, staples, or thumbstacks, and, presto, there's bonus storage space underneath. Slipcover or drape an old chair with the same fabric used to make the skirt. The one shown here has a ruffled pillow that ties on with a sash. If the table is in the bedroom and the bedroom is wallpapered, cover the top of the shelf with the same or a coordinating pattern and then put down a glass top. A stack of wire drawers on casters, readily available at most houseware stores, can be rolled under the shelf to keep perfume bottles, make-up jars, and the like out of sight. Just make sure you split the table skirt somewhere for easy access.

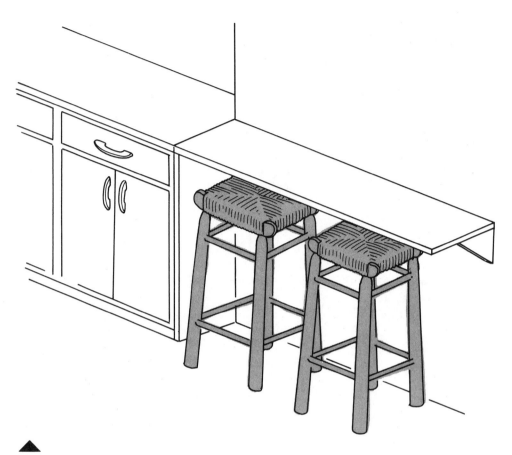

No place to grab a bite? Take a look at your kitchen. In almost every case you'll find a spot to install a breakfast shelf, which can also serve as extra counter space when it's not needed for eating. The shelf should be wide enough so you can shove a couple of stools underneath it and out of the way. Match the surface of the shelf to the counter surface, if possible, or use butcher block.

around before you settle on a particular style, and be sure the method you choose is sturdy enough to support not only the shelf but whatever you intend to put on it.

To prevent sagging, a shelf may need extra supports along its length at points other than where it's supported by brackets. If you're buying raw wood from a lumberyard, make sure it's properly seasoned, free of large knots that might drop out under the weight of what you're putting on the shelf, and of sufficient thickness (at least three-quarter inch) so it won't warp and sag. *Warning:* Marble and glass shelves are very heavy and may require expert installation.

12 LOFTY IDEAS

Sometimes the best way to double your space is to divide it horizontally—with a loft. Fashion photographers, artists, and bohemians are no longer the only ones taking advantage of this space-expanding idea. In fact, the only prerequisite is that your ceiling must be relatively high.

Exactly how high depends on the kind of loft you have in mind. In most cases, a sleeping loft requires the least amount of headroom—only about four feet—while a loft that accommodates someone sitting in a chair demands about five to six feet of clearance. Even then, most people will have to hunch over to stand. If you want to stand upright, you'll find seven feet of clearance is the minimum. Add to this figure the six and a half to seven feet needed below the loft, and you'll have an idea about just how high a ceiling you'll need.

There's more than one way to build a loft, however; some designs dramatically reduce the amount of headroom needed. For example, a sleeping loft can be installed over a desk or over a storage unit, neither of which needs a full seven feet of clearance. Lofts in children's rooms need less vertical space because you can take into account a child's height. Sleeping lofts have been built successfully above kitchenettes and even bathrooms.

NUTS AND BOLTS

There's a lot to think about before heading aloft. A loft and all the things you plan to put on it weigh a considerable amount. Can the floor take the load? If you're planning to use wall braces to hold up the loft, you must

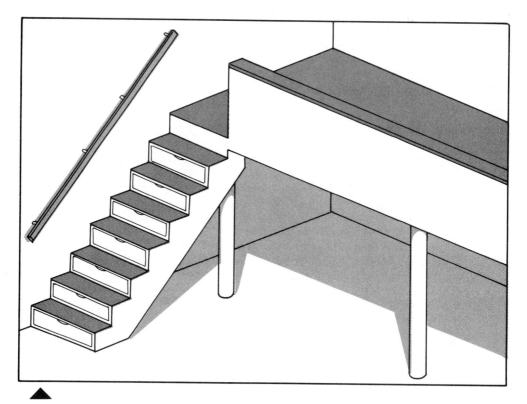

Here's a simple view of a basic loft that will adapt to many uses, including sleeping, depending on how much ceiling height you have to play with. The platform is braced against the wall and has individual columns for additional support. The traditional stairway has an unusual feature—a drawer is built into every riser. The area underneath the loft can be used for storage, an office, or a playroom. It all depends on the height of the loft.

find out how much weight the walls can safely bear. In general, unless you are an experienced builder, a loft is *not* a do-it-yourself project. Construction requires expert guidance, building permits, the go-ahead from your landlord (if you rent), and precise structural data.

The positioning of the loft is another matter that should not be left to chance. Your aim is to maximize your space without cutting off light and air circulation. You don't want to build a loft with a cave under it (unless you're going to use the space below for storage), so don't build a loft that obscures the light from your only window. It's best to position a loft against the wall opposite the window or windows, which allows light and air to reach both the upper and lower parts of the room.

SLEEPING ALOFT

Probably the most popular type is the sleeping loft, for several reasons. It frees up a large amount of floor space by moving the bed—a big space eater—up to another level. It eliminates the need to combine living and sleeping functions in a studio or to subdivide them. It also adds a significant amount of square footage while its ceiling-height requirement remains relatively modest.

The simplest sleeping loft consists of no more than a mattress, a bedside light, and some kind of ventilation in the form of an exhaust fan or a heat/air-conditioning duct. Ventilation is vital; because heat rises, a loft that is nice and cozy in winter may become unbearably stuffy in summer. You may decide to add an extra, such as carpeting, which will not only make the loft feel and look more luxurious but will also act as an excellent insulator and sound deadener. Depending on the amount of headroom you decide upon, your box spring may be able to accompany the mattress on the trip up. A major consideration is not to cut the space so close that you bang your head if you sit up in bed. If the vertical space available will barely accommodate a mattress, you might consider sleeping on futons. These cotton-filled mattresses of Japanese inspiration are ideal for lofts, and they don't need box springs to make them comfortable.

Book shelves, a low table, or some floor pillows, as well as baskets to hold your linens and extra blankets, are all nice additions to a sleeping loft if there's room for them. Bed making is simplified if you opt for a duvet-covered comforter because it only needs to be drawn up over the mattress to look good. Wall-mounted spots make excellent bedside lamps. You'll probably want to be able to turn off the upstairs lights from downstairs and vice versa, so make sure your plan includes conveniently located electrical outlets. While you're at it, you could design in remote controls for the stereo along with a set of speakers.

When you find yourself with sufficient vertical space, your options aren't limited to sleeping. An office, study, or library can be ensconced aloft, as can a reading area, a music listening room, or even a TV room. In fact, just about anything you'd like to move up a level can go except the dining room table, unless you're fond of carrying hot casseroles up ladders and stairs. Then again, a clever dumbwaiter or pulley system could make even that idea work. As for the grand piano. . .

IDEAS FOR DOWN UNDER

With more space to play with below now that you've moved some furniture "upstairs," weigh carefully the goings-on beneath the platform. Perhaps you'll choose more spacious living and just spread what's left into the void or, instead of keeping the space open, you could turn it into a

Not only does a loft add extra floor space, it transforms an uninteresting box-like room into a one-of-a-kind. The narrow loft platform shown here creates a home for an extensive library and, at the same time, injects a large dose of architectural interest into an otherwise ordinary room. Much of the impact is the result of using scavenged columns, antique stair rails, and so on, which have been incorporated into the design. At floor level, sliding cabinet doors conceal compartments for a television, a stereo, and a record collection. Works of art find a home among the books while more columns on the upper level create natural openings for paintings and prints.

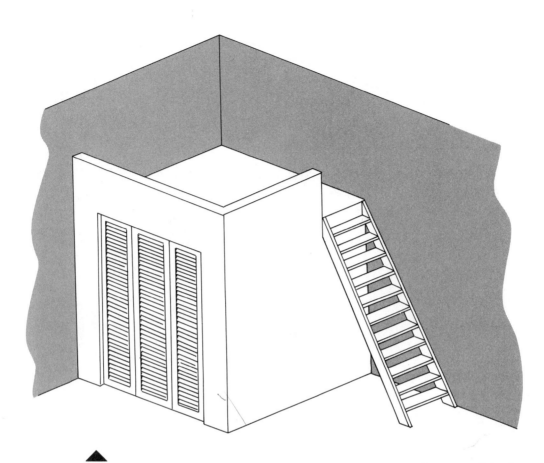

▲

Sometimes you'll want to close in the area under a loft bed. There are all kinds of things you can do with the new space. It could become a complete closet-cum-dressing room, an office, or a dark room, you could even consider making it a kitchen or bath, provided you can arrange the proper ventilation.

sleeping alcove that disappears behind doors or curtains by day. The same goes for a workshop or home office. If you're desperately short of shortage, you might choose to build closets underneath or a completely outfitted dressing room. It's your move.

HOW TO GET UP THERE

Something fun for children
- A rope ladder to ascend and a fireman's pole or a sliding board to descend
- A knotted rope for a young Tarzan

In a space-poor apartment, an unusual but convenient loft design is one built much like a bridge. It's certainly an option to consider when you have a long room where, for structural reasons, you are unable to situate a loft at either end. The upper level can house guest accommodations, your own bed, or a study, among other things. The space below makes a perfect dining area complete with a real "beamed" ceiling, which points naturally to a country look in furnishings. Access to this platform is provided by a circular stairway that adds its own charm.

- A pole with wooden crosspieces nailed to it
- A ladder on the perpendicular, secured to the side of the loft, and screwed into the floor

Something convenient for adults
- A prefabricated circular stair
- A rolling ladder on a track or library stairs
- Open riser stairs mounted to the side wall
- Closed riser stairs with built-in storage underneath

13 RESISTING THE APARTMENT SQUEEZE

Years ago someone in the real estate industry dreamed up the "½" room. You know—3½ rooms, central location, view of vacant lot. Puzzled apartment seekers soon learn that while a room has four walls, half a room does not. In fact, it doesn't have any walls to call its own. The "½" room is simply part of another larger room; the term is a euphemism that can't disguise the fact that a 3½-room apartment has one bedroom, no more.

While awaiting the advent of the "¼" room, renters are learning to live in the "½"—an apartment half the size, more or less, of the one they'd like to be living in. Unable to move, renters face both space limitations and boredom, wrought of being just plain sick and tired of living in the same old place.

The reaction of most people to apartment living has always been: "I'm only going to be here for a little while so why should I bother." The result has been the "brick-and-board-bookcase and wine-bottle-lamp" school of interior decorating. The unpleasant reality is that renters are now more likely than ever to live in the same apartment for several years. Once renters face that fact, they can also begin doing something about it.

Before starting any major overhaul, examine your lease so you know what you can and cannot do. There may be landlord's rules and regulations to be hurdled if you want to make an apartment feel bigger and more like a long-term home. Almost any type of construction will require the consent of the landlord, but landlords are often delighted if the improvements will increase the rental value of the apartment. Many buildings limit the number of colors you can paint an apartment; in other buildings the choices may be negotiable. Wallpapering is no longer a no-

no, since most wall coverings are strippable and can be removed in minutes without leaving a trace.

Many suggestions discussed elsewhere in this book will aid the apartment dweller in search of space, but some situations are unique to apartments.

THE MINUSCULE KITCHEN

If only the people who built the kitchens had to cook in them! New apartments are little better in this regard than older conversions where the kitchen has been squeezed into a shoe box. Start by installing shelves in every possible square inch to clear what little counter space has been provided for food preparation. Likely spots are over the refrigerator and around the doorway. When appliances are not built in there will be gaps between them. Fill in that space with small wooden or stainless-steel shelves, handy for spices and condiments. Put the inside of cabinet doors to work, especially those under the sink. Plastic holders and caddies that either screw into or glue onto the door can stash paper towels, food wrap, cleaning supplies, and more. Clip-on coated wire bins are handy catchalls inside cabinets or under open shelves. Beams or cleats on the ceiling, when equipped with hooks, can be used to store kitchen equipment. There are also any number of metal and wooden grids or iron racks to mount on the ceiling for this purpose. A kitchen windowsill can often be extended with a shelf for more counter space. It can be hinged to fold down and out of the way. Sometimes a small, drop-leaf table will fit in one end of a narrow kitchen. With stools tucked under it, the table can double as work and eating space. Don't overlook the tops of cabinets for storing bulky seldom-used items. Because this area attracts a lot of greasy cooking fallout, protect anything you store on cabinet tops in tins or baskets, the more decorative the better. If the kitchen sink happens to be an old one that's not built over a cabinet, skirt it with shirred fabric and hide your trash can or canned goods underneath.

THE BEDROOM

Apartment bedrooms, usually barely big enough to hold a bed, suffer from lack of space more than other rooms. Because bedrooms are out of the main traffic flow, they frequently double as storage rooms, with tenants squashing into them everything that won't fit elsewhere. Try substituting less furniture for more. Start with a headboard that incorporates storage for books, tissues, radio, and alarm clock. Wall-mounted lamps eliminate the need for bedside tables. A trunk at the foot of the bed can store bedding while providing seating and a perch for a television set as well.

A narrow, apartment kitchen will sometimes be just wide enough to accommodate a slim table that can be used for eating and as a much needed work surface. The table can be improvised out of a butcher block top and stock legs from a lumberyard. A used table with a drawer solves the problem of where to put silverware and cutlery; one with two drawers is even better. Don't waste the space above the table, either. Graduated shelves, wider at the top and narrower below, allow complete access to the table surface and lessen the danger of bumping your head in the cramped space.

Breaking the bed-against-the-wall habit may be hard to do, but it's well worth it when you consider the decorative possibilities. In a small bedroom, the walls are broken up by a closet and at least one door and one window, leaving very little choice when it comes to the positioning of the bed, which is, after all, the most important element in the room. Floating the bed in the center of the room changes the focus of the space as well as freeing the walls for art, shelves, built-in closets, or seating. In the room pictured here, inexpensive, campaign-style furniture—a desk at the head of the bed and a chest at the foot—provides work and storage space as well as that all-important something to lean against so your pillows don't fall on the floor. Pillows at both ends make the bed seem a bit more like a divan. The reasoning behind this setup was to free a wall for mirror-fronted closets, built by a clotheshorse who can't make do with the storage space that was provided. You can create your island bed from a simple carpet platform and mattress or a mattress alone, perhaps covered with a thick quilt. You could also use a boxspring and mattress combination and butt them against a drop-leaf table with one leaf down, or against the back of a blanket chest covered to match the bed, or against a fabric-skirted dressing table, or against a row of draped file cabinets topped with a piece of mirror, marble, or glass. Remember, if you want to have a lamp next to your bed, as opposed to overhead lighting, you must plan to have the wiring run under the area rug or through a seam in the wall-to-wall carpeting.

Floating the bed in the center of the room frees the periphery for other things. A bed placed lengthwise along a wall will not jut as far into the room; however, if the bed is for two, the person who sleeps on the inside may find this arrangement too confining. Modular wall units, if to your taste, are helpful in organizing bedroom clutter. High fourposter beds create instant storage underneath for suitcases, boxes of out-of-season clothes, and seldom needed files.

ENTRY HALLS AND FOYERS

It's not a room. It's not a hall. Maybe it's a vestibule. Mostly it's useless unless you really decide you must make this space pay off. Even a small foyer can hold a cabinet for bar supplies. Coat hooks and an umbrella stand produce an impromptu cloak room. Devise a dining spot for two with a long extra-narrow Parsons or drop-leaf table flanked by chairs— folding ones if necessary. A large foyer might accommodate a dining table for four or more. (Naturally, care should be taken to leave a passage so you don't have to climb over the diners.) An upright piano may fit in your foyer, or convert one wall of it into a floor-to-ceiling wine rack. A mirror will help dispel the gloom if the foyer is too dark, while a rogue's gallery of family photos can be an amusing way to greet visitors. Stripped, refinished, and mounted on the wall, the sash of an old, double-hung window, with the panes replaced with mirrors, can open the space by giving the illusion of an exterior view.

THE MAID'S ROOM

In the days when live-in help was far more common than it is now, many old apartments were built with maid's rooms. Maid's rooms are tiny, with correspondingly minute baths. If your lease and the building code permit, it may make sense to knock down the walls and join the maid's quarters to the adjacent room, especially because the adjoining room is frequently the kitchen. Maid's rooms have housed generations of second children, although it requires ingenuity to fit all the furniture and toys a child needs into such a confined space. Removing the old bath will increase the size of the room by about a third. If you decide against knocking down any walls, there are still other possibilities. The maid's room can become a den/TV room. A closet built in along the wall joining the bathroom would make an ideal laundry because all the necessary plumbing and a window to vent the dryer are at hand—in what used to be the maid's bathroom.

THE EXTRA BATH

If there is an underused second or third bathroom in which the toilet and sink are needed but the tub and shower are not, convert it into a powder

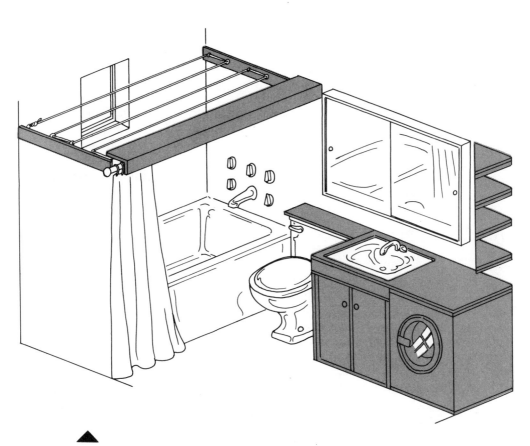

Apartments frequently have little or no space for a washer and dryer. If, after years of vegetating in a corner of the laundromat or reading *War and Peace* while waiting for a machine in the basement of your building, you simply can't take it anymore, a bathroom can often be rearranged to accommodate the equipment. To keep costs down, the best site is next to the basin or tub where the drainage lines and water pipes are located. You may have to move your sink over or get a smaller one. The machine will be less obtrusive if a laminate top is added that extends across the sink and the toilet tank (as shown here). (The toilet tank section should be removable so you can open the tank when necessary.) If it's impossible to vent a dryer, a quite satisfactory indoor line-drying system can be rigged over the bath. In this system, wood cleats are affixed to the walls at shower-rod height, and a clothesline is threaded through screw eyes mounted at intervals on cleats. It all can be hidden by a baffle that also conceals the shower rod.

room/storage room. Conceal a shelf system or a hanging rod with an opaque shower curtain. You can also convert the bath to temporary infant's quarters by covering the tub with plywood, then shirring a skirt around it for the bassinet to sit on. Curtains hung from the shower rod and tied back on either side make a pretty, cozy alcove.

HALLWAYS

Some hallways are wide enough to line with bookcases. Consider a picture gallery for a narrow hall. An occasional odd nook or jog in the wall will hold a small chest of drawers. Build a closet across the end of a hall that deadends. A very wide hall works well as an auxiliary sitting room but may need a screen to define it and give it some intimacy. Move in the piano, and you have a music room.

THE LIVING ROOM

Most apartment dwellers cannot afford a living room that is strictly for show. An apartment living room should be comfortable and inviting enough that you use it daily. Invest your money in a few good pieces of furniture, such as a well-made sofa and a couple of versatile chairs that will fit in any house or apartment, not just the one you're living in now. Update the look from time to time with fabric and accessories—a much cheaper way of going about redecorating than buying new furniture. On special occasions you can dress up the room with silk pillows, flowers, candles, a lace topper on a skirted table, or an arrangement of favorite things not usually massed together.

BUYING FURNITURE

The best philosophy is: You *can* take it with you when you go. Don't spend a lot of money on a combination magazine rack/TV table/hot plate fit only for a specific apartment unless you absolutely love this particular piece of furniture. When shopping for sleep sofas, remember that the best-quality ones will hold up the longest; most can be reupholstered, and many can be slipcovered. In fact, you can change the look of any sofa by varying the pillow size and shape—simply wrap the pillow forms with sheets of fiberfill or foam before covering them with the new fabric. Drop-leaf tables look natural in both open and closed states but some collapsible furniture does not. Pedestal tables take up less room visually and have no legs to interfere with chairs drawn up around them. Whenever possible, let each piece of furniture do more than one thing without seeming to do so—a coffee table/vitrine, a bedside table/desk, a skirted table/file cabinet.

Open shelving is one of the most versatile of dividers and is ideally suited to apartment living. With the addition of a leaf to drop down or lift up, the unit also substitutes for a dining table and/or desk. Filling the shelves attractively is a must. Whether your look is a few scattered objets d'art or a lot of creative clutter, there has to be some plan or the whole thing becomes an eyesore instead of an asset. Don't forget the divider is viewed from both sides. Row upon row of stacked book pages are not very attractive and should be broken up by ornaments, or the shelves should be wide enough to hold two rows facing each other so that only the spines are visible from either side. Try filling individual shelves with groupings of similar objects—teapots, blue and white stoneware, all your souvenirs, or baskets. You'll be surprised what you can pull together if you rummage around; many objects, not substantial enough to make much of an impression alone, become far more decorative when grouped—graters, toast racks, candlesticks, frogs, and so forth.

BUILT-INS

These are expensive but wonderfully economical when it comes to space. You must have a designer, and you can't cut corners. The quality of materials and workmanship is as important as the design. What's the use of the latest in cabinetry if the laminate unlaminates, the drawers stick, and the doors warp? Discuss with the designer how many of the built-in units can be moved when you do. And make sure you like the look; a lot of built-ins project a certain feeling, quite deliciously sleek, but too much so for some tastes.

14 STUDIO STRATEGIES

No matter how you look at it, a studio apartment is *one room.* If you're lucky, yours is large, sunny, and high ceilinged. If you're not, you may be calling something not much bigger—or better—than a roach motel home. Regardless of size, most studios have one thing in common: there's no place to go. There's also an acute lack of storage space followed immediately by inadequate kitchen facilities. Studios are a terrific challenge to your ingenuity if you want something more than a living room with a fold-out couch.

The first thing to do is go through your possessions and discard as many things as possible. Don't try to fit everything you own into a one-room apartment. If there was ever a time to get rid of a lot of high school and college junk, this is it. Some things, too precious to part with permanently, might find a home in the attic of a compassionate relative or friend until your circumstances permit moving into larger quarters.

One of the best ways to deal with a studio apartment is to build a platform or a loft (see Chapter 12, "Lofty Ideas"). Lofts provide what amounts to another room, freeing the space below for a real living room, a living room/office, or a number of other combinations. Platforms, although they don't create additional square footage, do help subdivide a room into separate living areas. It's amazing how effectively a step or two up or down gives the impression that you've got someplace else to go.

FURNITURE

Choosing furniture for a studio apartment is a tricky proposition. A room full of dinky, small-scale pieces is strictly for pygmies. Mix in a couple of

▶

Combining home and office in this small studio was made somewhat easier because behind the bifold doors there's a sleeping alcove to house the bed. Even so, the owner needed to create a reasonable facsimile of a living room and dining room and still have space for an office. The work area takes over the end of the room nearest the windows, with one side of the desk acting as a back for the couch. A Japanese screen cuts off the view to the front door and kitchenette. The sofa and chair form a satisfactory conversation area, while a wheeled serving cart substitutes for a coffee table and can be pushed out of the way when desired. The dining table at the far end doubles as a conference table. The room's decor combines high-tech and no-tech design—practical filing cabinets, chrome chairs, and laminate surfaces mix naturlaly with wicker, a country oak desk and chair, and a few well-chosen accessories.

One way to make a long narrow room seem less like a bowling alley is to build a platform across one end, preferably the end where the window is situated. The seating area shown here is also a sleeping platform, designed with storage cubbies in the base and covered with tatami mats, flat woven straw mats. The "sofa" is simply a futon in its sitting position that pulls flat at night to make a double bed. The entire area can be blocked off by lowering the center bamboo shade which, along with the two narrow ones on either side, creates a dramatic proscenium effect.

larger things to avoid having a wall-to-wall, pint-sized look. Include at least one tall piece that raises the eye to the ceiling and takes advantage of vertical space. To relieve whatever closet space you've got of some of its burden, select furnishings with storage capacity. An antique trunk gives you storage space and serves as a coffee table or bedside table as well. An armoire adds a sense of dignity to a room and provides instant

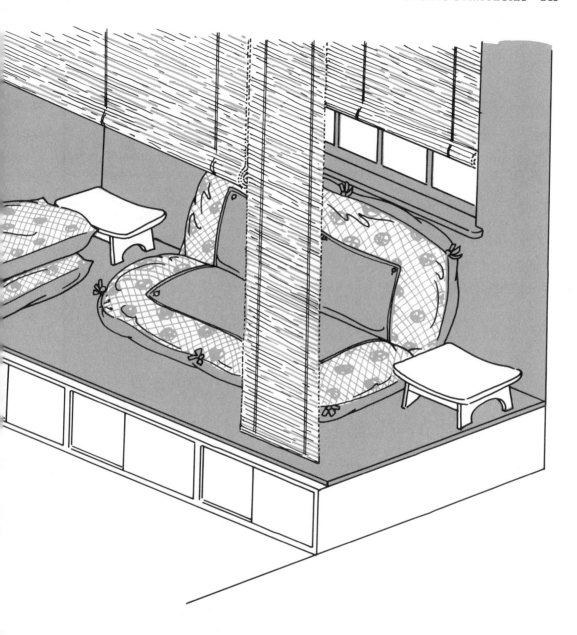

closet space. Depending on how the armoire is constructed, you may be able to store things on top of it, too. Even ottomans are made with removable tops, leaving room inside for storing candlesticks, place mats, napkin holders, and the like. You can ease more of the crunch by storing your out-of-season clothes at the dry cleaners, a service most offer at reasonable rates.

WHERE TO SLEEP

Just what form your sleeping accommodations take is one of the most important decisions you'll have to make. If your studio has a loft or an alcove or if it's L-shaped, you can usually arrange it so a traditional bed—or at least a good-sized mattress—will fit right in. There's a psychological advantage to having a real bed; it makes one-room living feel less of a sacrifice. If your bed must double as daytime seating, you can disguise it in various ways, the least expensive of which is with a tailored slipcover and pillows. Another good solution is to raise the mattress on a platform or build a platform with a well in it so the mattress is hidden in the well, like a sunken bathtub. While neither way actually saves space, both help isolate the sleeping area. The "sunken idea" almost hides the bed completely and adds an interesting seating feature that could eliminate the need for a sofa. The Murphy bed, which folds down from the wall and is concealed in its own storage unit, means you can have a real bed in a room and never know it's there (see Chapter 9, "The Guesting Game"). While you could install a Murphy bed in a closet, there's no need to take up valuable storage space since most systems are no deeper than average wall units and are designed to be installed flush against the wall.

Some people prefer the sofa bed, which has both pluses and minuses. One advantage is that you won't be trying to fit both a bed and a sofa in the same undersized room. One disadvantage is that you have a certain amount of rearranging to do every time you go to bed. Futons, the Japanese answer to the Castro convertible (see Chapter 9, "The Guesting Game"), are relatively inexpensive and comfortable for both sitting and sleeping. However, they demand a proclivity toward floor-level living.

Manufacturers have come up with any number of cleverly designed units, impossible to enumerate here, with beds that pull out or drop down. You can find them everywhere from "to-the-trade" showrooms to the Sears catalogue (see source listings beginning on page 167).

WINNING THE SPACE WAR

One approach to the studio apartment is to separate it into specific areas—one for working, one for sleeping, one for relaxing and entertaining. Breaking up the space—or rearranging it—helps give the impression that you have more than one room to live in. Movable dividers, such as decorative folding screens, flexible lighting, and furniture with casters, help you increase the degree of separation when you want to.

While you do want to divide a small apartment into distinct living areas, keep the decorating scheme unified. An overall design adds some sophistication. It harmonizes a room that is broken up into different areas and keeps it from looking fragmented. Use the same colors or fabrics and their variations in each area. If you have one fabric on the sofa and another on the side chairs, use the second fabric for a table skirt or the bedspread in the sleeping area. The many coordinated groups of fabrics, wall coverings, and even paint colors now available make this sort of unified decorating easier than ever.

Mirrors, though hardly a new idea for studios, shouldn't be passed over, because they help dispel gloom and banish the feeling that the walls are closing in on you. A mirror on the wall opposite a window will almost double the light the window affords. Mirroring the window reveals (the indented area between the inside surface of the wall and the window frame) brings in pretty reflections. When covering a full wall with mirrors, be sure to include any door to give the impression of one unbroken expanse. Think of putting mirrors on the back of a room divider or around a square pillar. A mirror behind open shelving makes it seem as though there's another room behind the plates and glasses. Even kitchen backsplashes look deeper when they're mirrored.

So that you don't find yourself trying to read by the light of a glaring overhead bulb, install fixtures that are as flexible as possible. Carefully think out the kind of lighting you'll need in your working, sleeping, and entertaining areas. The best lighting is adjustable. Floor lamps that can be raised or lowered, wall-mounted lamps on adjustable arms, and small spots that can be used on a table top or on the floor are good choices for studios. Remember that lamps with opaque lamp shades shed more directional light than lamps with translucent silk or paper shades. The latter produce a more diffuse glow and illuminate some of the room as well. Install dimmers for a quick change of mood as well as a way to save money. (They reduce the amount of electricity used.) If your studio has a platform, you might consider installing a fluorescent tube under a baffle along the edge. This will make the platform appear to float. In a particularly cavelike studio, you can fake a skylight by dropping the center of the ceiling and adding soft lights behind a grid of translucent white panels or behind a section of stained glass.

ENTERTAINING IN ONE ROOM

Admittedly, entertaining is difficult in a studio, but if you're resourceful, it can still be a lot of fun. Make sure there's some way to shut off the view of the kitchen area so the messy preparations don't intrude on the festivities. A hinged screen, a curtain, or a venetian blind will do. Spotlighting the entertainment area and leaving the rest in the dark has the same effect.

Use your coffee table as a dining table or buffet. You can even buy a model that adjusts to three heights: coffee, continental, and dining. If you

A lot can be done to make a very small studio liveable, even if your budget is smaller than the room. A bed with a storage base on one side of the room and a loveseat on the other make up quite a comfortable conversation grouping. The little end table to the left of the loveseat has a drop leaf and can be placed in the center of the room for informal dining. A shelf that runs the length of the room, even over the door, provides visible storage space, and a partition between the bed and the door can be curtained to make a dressing area.

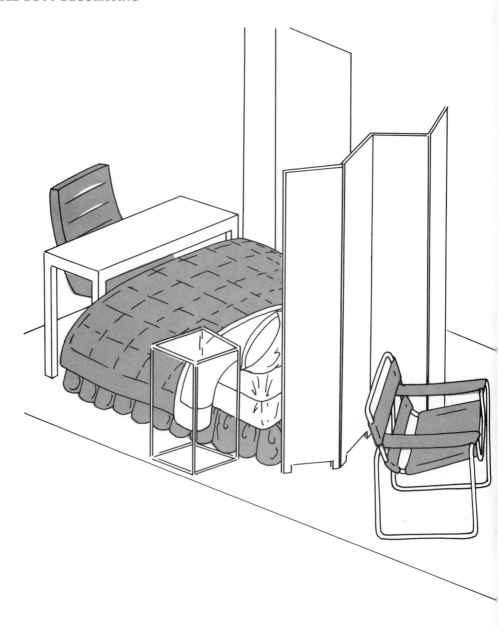

don't have a coffee table, make one from an ottoman topped with a large shallow basket. With oversized pillows all the decorating rage these days, you can use the ones on your sofa as floor cushions for informal dining Japanese-style. Twenty-three-inch squares of Dacron-wrapped foam look great in fabric covers with Turkish corners. For more ideas on entertaining with limited facilities, see Chapter 3, "Living Rooms with More."

In an L-shaped studio, the obvious place for the bed is usually in the short leg of the L. In the example shown here, a folding screen divides the sleeping area from the living area and functions as a headboard for the bed at the same time. At the foot of the bed is a Parsons desk; aside from providing work space, it can hold the telephone and the TV. The seating and dining areas are separated by a chrome and glass étagère, which allows one area to be seen from the other and doesn't block the light. A bookcase would be a more emphatic alternative. The seating arrangement, which includes an L-shaped sofa and a Breuer chair, handles four people comfortably. The uncluttered modern decor contributes to the feeling of open space.

15 DESIGNING FOR THE DOUBLE LIFE

The days when an interior designer wouldn't touch a room smaller than the Superdome are over. Many of today's designers not only deal with small spaces, they specialize in them, and well they might. With clients expecting miracles, the designer often needs to produce the decorating equivalent of "the loaves and the fishes," creating many rooms out of one. The amazing part is that the designers frequently succeed. Most interior decorators develop highly individual ways of dealing with small spaces. They mix good looks with the necessities of life, and they manage to do it without sacrificing either comfort or excitement.

The following assemblage of bright young designers has agreed to let you in on some of their decorating secrets. Most of the designers do all kinds of jobs—large and small. All have put a considerable amount of thought into the space question and have come up with quite different personal approaches for dealing with it.

COBUILD ASSOCIATES

Paul Schaefer and Jean Weiner of Cobuild Associates, a young New York architectural firm, specialize in doing the impossible. "When people come to us, they've finally given up on their furniture," says Weiner. "Usually they've reached the state where they want to get rid of it all. The very fact they come to us means they're ready for something different."

The designers apply a two-part philosophy to every job. They use standard ready-made pieces along with custom-built elements to reduce

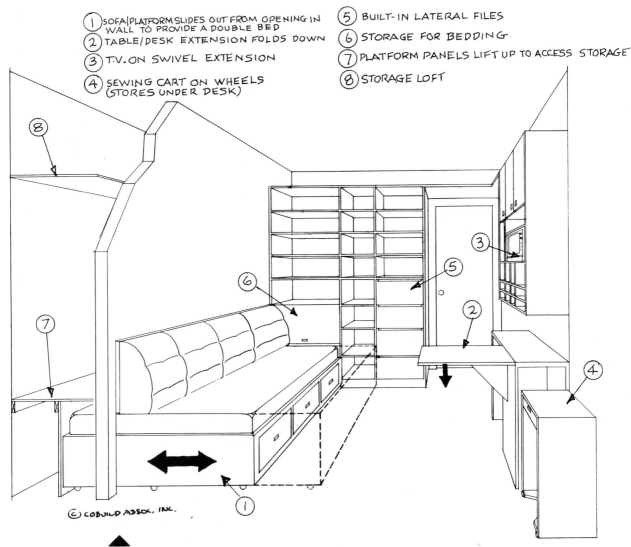

1. SOFA/PLATFORM SLIDES OUT FROM OPENING IN WALL TO PROVIDE A DOUBLE BED
2. TABLE/DESK EXTENSION FOLDS DOWN
3. T.V. ON SWIVEL EXTENSION
4. SEWING CART ON WHEELS (STORES UNDER DESK)
5. BUILT-IN LATERAL FILES
6. STORAGE FOR BEDDING
7. PLATFORM PANELS LIFT UP TO ACCESS STORAGE
8. STORAGE LOFT

© COBUILD ASSOC, INC.

▲

Typical of the work Jean Weiner and Paul Schaefer of Cobuild Associates are called on to do is this four-in-one family room/house office/work room/guest room that measures nine feet by twelve feet. The elements fit together like pieces of a jigsaw puzzle. The sofa bed is on a platform with three storage drawers which slides out of an opening in the wall to form a double bed. (The space on the other side was snatched from a closet.) Across from the sofa is the desk unit, which consists of a table flush to the wall with an extension that lifts up to provide the ideal L-shaped work surface. Above the desk, amid cubbyholes and cabinets, is the TV, mounted on a sliding extension that swivels so the set can be viewed from anywhere in the room. Under the right side of the desk is a sewing cart on wheels, shown here pulled out. The far wall is covered floor to ceiling with shelves into which have been built four lateral files and a storage cabinet for bedding.

costs, and they design things that can be taken and moved to the client's next apartment.

Clients are asked to list all the things they want to do in a particular room—sleeping, eating, tap dancing, building a canoe. "Most of the time everything can be accommodated except a king-size bed and two desks," says Schaefer. "It's usually easier than you think. Most people have already figured out their alternatives but just can't seem to follow through."

Weiner and Schaefer like to keep things movable. They have designed couches that slide into bookcases, cubes on casters, tables that pull down from the wall, and beds that descend from the ceiling. "But we make sure that all these things are easy to use. The mechanics have to be simple," they point out.

The Cobuild message is that life can be fun, even in an undersized apartment. "Remember the way you felt when you were a kid and you liked climbing a ladder to get into the top bunk?" says Schaefer. "We're trying to recapture the same spirit on an adult scale."

SUSAN ZISES GREEN

Susan Zises Green has found a way to incorporate her big decorating ideas—fabulous rugs and wonderful walls—into small spaces. She also loves bright colors and exciting fabrics.

"I like large furniture in a small-scale room," Green says. "Not everything, of course, but you need something distinguished or the room will look too insignificant." Her usual method for attaining this is to buy one or two pieces of the best upholstered furniture in a simple, untrendy style.

"The seating in a small room must be multifunctional, so, for example, I always make sure a sofa bed is large enough to nap on comfortably without unfolding it," Green says. Another good choice along these lines is a club chair that is big enough to curl up in. Her favorite sofa bed style has softly rounded arms and a high back, and she has them custom-made for a fraction above department store prices. "They're worth it because they last much longer," she says.

Green is not opposed to cutting corners, however. She believes the place to save money is on fabric—not upholstery fabric, which must be durable, but fabric for slipcovers, curtains, table drapes, and so on. "These things don't have to last forever so you can change the whole look with a new fabric from time to time," she says.

JEFFREY WEISS

Jeffrey Weiss believes that while most people are very conscious of the way they look, they tend to be oblivious to the message their environment

In an apartment with not a corner to spare for an overnight guest, Susan Zises Green made do with the only space she could find—the small dining area behind a galley kitchen. The space, which is normally the breakfast room, converts into workable sleeping quarters because the seating unit folds out into a bed. The table is on slides and is easily pushed out of the way. A sliding door separates the room from the kitchen for privacy; a wall of mirrors makes the whole area seem larger. The floor is painted in a veritable rainbow of color to match the sofa, which is slipcovered for easy cleaning.

is sending out about them. It's one of the reasons he starts almost every job with the closets—to get the junk and the clutter out of sight.

"I've never seen a closet that does a good job," says Weiss, referring to the standard, single rod arrangement most builders have provided since time immemorial. Weiss puts more than one rod in a closet, along with lots of shelving, all kinds of hooks, and sometimes even a dresser. One of his favorite ways of dealing with a client's possessions is to keep them stacked in transparent plastic shoe boxes on shelves in the closet. "What's the use of having things if you don't remember they're there?" he asks reasonably. While Weiss has custom closet work done for many of his clients, he loves inexpensive closet organizer systems, such as the one by Rubbermaid, which he uses frequently.

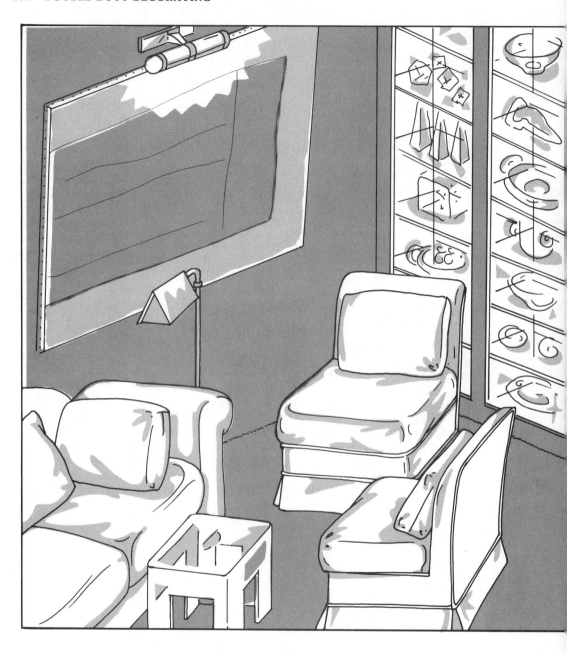

Jeffrey Weiss favors a dining room banquette arrangement, a solution that saves space without sacrificing ambiance. In fact, a banquette does more than save space: it allows you to push the table into a corner without pulling it out for every meal, and it offers great storage in the wells under the seats. Weiss usually chooses a dining table slightly lower than the norm so that living room side chairs, whose seats are often closer to the floor, can be used at the table. Comfort is the key for this designer, who believes in creating a dining space so pleasant that people will wish to linger. Lighting plays a part in this—recessed spots over the table are controlled by dimmers while picture lights highlight the art and provide a general background glow.

Well-organized closets are essential in the bedroom; Weiss thinks this is the most important room in the house. "You should be able to eat there, watch TV there, as well as read and sleep," he says. He begins with a bed and a desk. By making the closet super efficient and eliminating some of the usual bedroom furniture—say, the night tables and/or the dresser—Weiss has opened up enough space in the room for an armoire, a chaise, or a loveseat, all of which are far more interesting and serve many more purposes than the standard bedroom pieces.

In addition, Weiss says, rooms should be "multiambient." You shouldn't lock yourself into one look with inflexible possessions. In cramped apartments, he prefers small-scale, simply styled furniture. He then creates excitement with oversized accessories (big, fat candles, substantial pillows, large vases) and unusual and varied lighting (an indirect light shining on a massed group of plants, recessed spots over a dining area, traditional lamps in one area and track lighting in another). With very little effort his spaces turn playful, businesslike, romantic, or homey.

Even in the smallest rooms, Weiss leaves space for something purely pretty—a grouping of antique books, a vase of roses, or a daguerreotype. "Don't always put things in obvious places," he says. "Put art in the bathroom, a pomander in the closet. Give the viewer an unexpected and pleasant surprise." It's a dimension every space can have, no matter how small.

SCOTT KEMPER

For Scott Kemper of Dallas, making it pretty is the easy part; it's finding the right design that's the challenge. Even in this Texas city where lack of space is not usually a problem, more and more of his younger clients are becoming unwilling to sink every cent they have into one large house. "They prefer to have the flexibility that allows them another life—a cabin in the country, for example, as well as a place in town—which means that some rooms have to be used for more than one thing," Kemper says.

His dining room/office is a fine example of the way he attacks the problem. "Everything in the room is either on casters or is light enough to be lifted out of the way," he says. At the end of the working day, the "non-dining" elements are either shoved or rolled to the perimeter.

The table is the center of the room and happens to be something special—Danish Art Deco—but it could be any well-designed table. "And it's multifunctional—all flat-topped surfaces are multifunctional," Kemper points out. Over the table hangs a pendant lamp that pulls up and down and is equipped with a rheostat for dimming. The other lighting is equally flexible: a photographer's lamp on a stand that can be beamed up and down; pin-up spots that can be aimed up to act like sconces or down when more work light is needed.

"The window treatment is young, easy, and removable," says Kemper. The windows are fitted with aluminum blinds and then softened with a simple drapery treatment. "It's just three yards of fabric folded over a rod, tucked, and pinned back. With the draperies, the room looks softer; without them, it looks cleaner."

Kemper's multifunctional approach can be applied to more than just residential interiors. "In junior executive-level offices I find myself having to combine office, reception, and conference areas in one space," he says. "I'm doing it by mixing residential and functional pieces—and making those with a purely office function removable."

ROBERT LONE

Bob Lone knows that people expect a lot, even when they don't have a lot to work with. To start, he divides studio apartments into entertaining, sleeping, and task areas. "Everyone needs a desk and a bookcase," he points out. When the sleeping and entertaining areas are one and the same, Lone considers both comfort and ambience. "I make sure there's a proper reading light and tables to put things on nearby, after the guests have gone," he says.

Although he describes himself as "not at all a minimalist," Lone feels it's terribly important for furnishings to have a certain amount of space around them. "Furniture needs to breathe. It shouldn't be pushed together. It's like finding the right size mat for a watercolor," he says. Lone should know; he has directed two art galleries.

According to Lone, a sense of order increases the illusion of spaciousness, which puts a high priority on creating specific places for your possessions. "In small apartments the need for storage is enormous," says Lone, "but there are ways to do it without feeling closed in by wall upon wall of cabinets." He chooses wall units that incorporate lots of mirrors—mirrors behind the shelves or on the doors, for example—which not only make the unit more interesting to look at but increase the illusion of spaciousness, too. He frequently calls in a carpenter to give freestanding wall units a built-in look by adding a soffit at the top and moldings around the edges.

Lone also makes use of reflective surfaces throughout small apartments. He likes mirror, brass, silver, glass, and lacquer because they bounce light back and forth; they fill a static room with life.

As for the cost, Lone knows that decorating can be an expensive undertaking, making it doubly important to choose classic and durable pieces that your eyes won't tire of. "But if you added up the cost of everything in your linen closet, you'd probably be shocked at the total," he says. "It just seems like less because you didn't have to buy it all at the same time, the way you must purchase the contents of a room."

Scott Kemper took advantage of nicely designed functional pieces and combined them with bentwood chairs and an Art Deco table in his studio/dining room. The molded plastic module holds his phone and design supplies and rolls to the corner at the end of the day; the chairs are simply rearranged around the table. A white file cabinet (lower right) holds three horizontal file drawers and doesn't intrude into the room. The top level can be converted into a bar. Lighting includes an adjustable pendant lamp, a photographer's lamp on a stand, and pin-up spots (not shown) on the file cabinet wall. The draperies are folded panels of fabric tacked to the side with push pins.

In a living room with limited space, Bob Lone used the island effect to separate the dining area from the rest of the room. The main seating is centered on an Oriental rug surrounded by bare wood floors. An armless sofa with a chaise at each end also acts as a subtle divider. Although quite spacious, this grouping can seat two intimately or larger groups comfortably. In the dining area, Lone positioned the table against the wall so that four people can dine— two on one side, one on each end—without moving the table. When the table is pulled from the wall to accommodate six people, the owners use two matching chairs at the other end of the room (not shown) for extra seating. A series of laminate cubes, shown here lined up and holding plants, can be stacked into a pedestal when desired. Both chaises are big enough to sleep an occasional overnight guest.

ROBERT S. HART

Robert Hart has become an expert on small apartments, his own having provided a lot of first-hand experience. "My clients almost always ask for multiuse rooms and I'm finding that, no matter what the budget, everyone is desperate for space," he says.

The traditional sofa bed solution in a studio apartment is not one of Hart's favorites. "I don't really like sofa beds because they're so unattrac-

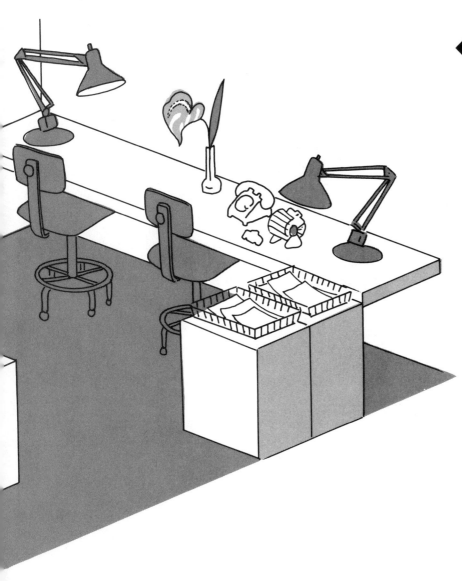

This bedroom belongs to a graphics designer who demanded the maximum amount of work surface; Robert Hart provided it with the minimum amount of custom carpentry. The main desk, topped in white laminate, spans the room under the windows. A long Parsons table, also laminated in white, runs the length of the queen-sized bed. Hart also supplied open industrial wire shelving and two white file cabinets. Three artist's lamps on flexible arms furnish all the illumination necessary; one of them is positioned to swing over to the bed for nighttime reading. The base of the bed is actually made of huge multidrawered flat files for storing the owner's work. The bed itself has a fitted spread and tailored contour pillows in keeping with the business-like atmosphere, but they're done in deep jewel colors to offset the relative austerity of the room.

tive when they're sitting open. I only use them as a last resort." Instead he prefers to transform a full-size bed into a sofa by piling pillows along the back or down the center. "I'll sacrifice a foot of space elsewhere to have room for a double bed," he says. "I think it's the civilized size for one person."

The trick of piling pillows down the center of the bed creates a sort of two-sided couch, which is handy particularly when the bed is in the center of the room. Hart chooses pillows covered in coarse textured fabrics and filled with kapok. Their heavy weight gives them stability, as does the fabric, which prevents them from slipping against each other and sliding onto the floor.

When it comes to color, Hart leans toward either pale or dark monochromatic combinations, which he feels work best in small spaces. He also uses a minimum of patterns, because he feels they cause visual clutter. "Certainly, if you have a bed and a sofa in the same room, they should be in the same fabric," he adds.

Hart favors furniture that can be rearranged for entertaining. An ottoman is used alone or with a chair to form a chaise. Pillows move from the sofa to the floor for seating. Two lacquer tables make a coffee table when used together and end or occasional tables when used apart. Sofa units change from an L-shaped configuration to a pit or are arranged into two facing loveseats. Hart likes to change the look frequently. He has even gone so far as to frame a mirror between two pilasters for a client who desperately needed the illusion of another room in his studio apartment. It looks exactly like a door.

DESIGNERS

Scott Kemper Design
2721 Cedar Springs, Suite #7
Dallas, TX 75201

Susan Zises Green, A.S.I.D.
500 East 77 Street
New York, NY 10021

Robert Lone Interiors
151 East 83 Street
New York, NY 10028

Jeffrey Weiss Design, Inc.
233 East 54 Street
New York, NY 10022

Jean Weiner and Paul Schaefer
Cobuild Associates
2112 Broadway, Room 209
New York, NY 10023

Robert S. Hart Interior Design
237 East 54 Street
New York, NY 10022

RESOURCE LIST

In addition to stores and dealers near you, you may want to investigate the following sources, all of which offer catalogs and brochures by mail. Those companies that do not sell directly to consumers will usually include a list of dealers where their products can be found.

HOME FURNISHINGS

Conran's
145 Huguenot Street
New Rochelle, NY 10801
$2 for quarterly catalog

Workbench
470 Park Avenue
New York, NY 10016
$2 for catalog

Castro Convertibles
1990 Jericho Turnpike
New Hyde Park, NY 11040

Sears Roebuck Company
Catalog Division
4640 Roosevelt Boulevard
Philadelphia, PA 19132

Laura Ashley
Homefurnishings
Dept. 51, Box 5308
Melville, NY 11747
$4 for catalog

The Children's Room
318 East 45 Street
New York, NY 10017
$1 for catalog

J.C. Penney Company
PO Box 2056
Milwaukee, WI 53201

Room Plus
1555 Third Avenue
New York, NY 10028

HOUSEWARES

Horchow Collection
Practicalities
PO Box 340257
Dallas, TX 75234

Brookstone
Housewares Catalog
127 Vose Farm Road
Peterborough, NH 03458

JAPANESE HOME FURNISHINGS

Miya Shoji
107 East 17 Street
New York, NY 10011
Screens and tatami mats

Arise Futon Mattress Company
37 Wooster Street
New York, NY 10013
$2 for catalog

The Futon Shop
178 West Houston Street
New York, NY 10014

MURPHY BEDS, WALL SYSTEMS, KITCHENS

Lew Raynes Murphy Beds
40 East 34 Street
New York, NY 10016
50 cents for catalog

Murphy Bed and Kitchen
  Company
40 East 34 Street
New York, NY 10016

Lockwood Furniture Systems
1187 Third Avenue
New York, NY 10028

CLOSET SYSTEMS

Clairson International (formerly
  Closet Maid)
Consumer Products Division
720 Southwest 17 Street
Ocala, FL 32670

Closet King
430 East 72 Street
New York, NY 10021

Rubbermaid Inc.
1147 Akron Road
Wooster, OH 44691

LIGHTING

Progress Lighting
Advertising Dept.
G Street and Erie Avenue
Philadelphia, PA 19134
$1 for catalog

Rosetta Electric
21 West 46 Street
New York, NY 10036

MISCELLANEOUS

Putnam Rolling Ladder
32 Howard Street
New York, NY 10013
All kinds of ladders

Scandia Down Shops
1040 Industry Drive
Seattle, WA 98188
Bedding
$2 for catalog

Sam Flax
111 Eighth Avenue
New York, NY 10011
*Art supplies and related
    furnishings*
$3 for catalog

American Wood Column
    Corporation
913 Grand Street
Brooklyn, NY 11211
Moldings, turnings, columns

Mylen Stairs
650 Washington Street
Peekskill, NY 10566
Circular and open riser stairs
50 cents for catalog

Kartell USA
225 Fifth Avenue
New York, NY 10010
Plastic storage items, stackables

Noise Control Products
1468 West 9 Street
Cleveland, OH 44113
*Decorative acoustical panels and
    paneling*

Puckihuddle Products
Oliverea, NY 12462
Crafts, accessories, and bedding
$1 for catalog

INDEX

apartments, small, 130–138
audiovisual centers, in bedrooms, 42; in dining rooms, 35; in kitchens, 60–61
audiovisual equipment, 19, 42, 58–59, 60–61, 74; in closets, 102; on lofts, 125

baby care centers, in closets, *103*
bars, in closets, *104;* in kitchens, 61
bathrooms, 134, *135;* under lofts, *127*
bedrooms, 40–47, *48–49;* as audiovisual centers, 42; as clothes storage, *47;* as gyms, 44–46; insulating of, 46, 48; lighting of, 48–49; as office spaces, *82–83;* as sitting rooms, 40, *41,* 42, *44–45;* small, 131, *133;* soundproofing of, 46–48; as studios, 40, *162–163; see also* lofts
beds, in alcoves, *43;* bunk, *64, 67,* 69, 82; canopy, *71;* in center of room, *133;* children's, 70, *71;* folding, *88;* fourposter, *44–45,* 84; loft, 66, *67,* 68, *127;* Murphy, 85, *90–91;* in office spaces, *82–83,* 84–85; on platforms, 66, *151;* rollaway, 88; trundle, 65, 69, 92;

blinds, for alcoves, *84;* matchstick, 31; as room dividers, *80–81;*
building permits for lofts, 124
built-in units, 138

cabinets, bedside, 42; file, 36, 40, 74, 77–78; kitchen, 56; old-time wooden, 57; table linen, 57; wall-mounted, 42
carpeting, on platforms, 7; as room dividers, *11;* for insulating and soundproofing, 46–47; wall-to-wall, 19, 46–47, 65
ceilings, soundproofing of, 48
chairs, beanbag, 19; club, 40; convertible, 33, *88;* desk, 77; folding, *88;* side, 40; slip covering of, 19; stackable, *27*
chaises longues, *41*
chests, 70; built-in, *76;* as room dividers, *10*
children's areas in dining rooms, 18
children's furniture, 19, 65–68
children's rooms, 63, *64,* 65–74; shelves in, *119*
closets, 16, 36, *47,* 95–105, 153, 156; as baby care centers, *103;* as bars, *104;* construction of, 97; design and

renovation of, 95–97, *96;* as clothes storage, 102; with dressing tables, *96;* for desks, *98;* for gardening equipment, *101;* as hobby areas, 102; as laundries, 97, *100;* location of, 97; under lofts, 127; as office spaces, *84–85, 98;* as pantries, 102; as powder rooms, 102; for saunas, 102; as sewing centers, *84, 99;* as telephone booths, 97, 102; triangular, 97; under-the-stairs, 105–106; as wine cellars, 105; as workshops, 105

clothes storage, 70; in bedrooms, *47;* for children, 65, 70; in closets, 102

Cobuild Associates, 150, *151,* 152

computers, 59; in kitchens, 61; in office spaces, 77

conference rooms, *80–81;* and dining rooms in living rooms *28–29*

counterspace, on shelves *122;* in kitchens, *57*

curtains for insulating and soundproofing, 46

dens, in dining rooms, *34–35,* 36; and dining rooms in kitchens, *54–55, 58–59;* as office spaces, *76*

desks, 26; for children, *119;* in closets, *98;* as dining tables, 4; drop-front, 42; Parsons, 33; partners, 74

dining alcoves in kitchens, *53*

dining rooms, 32–39; with children's areas, 18; and conference rooms in living rooms *28–29;* as dens, *34–35,* 36; and dens in kitchens, *54–55, 58–59;* as keeping rooms *38–39;* as libraries, 33; in living rooms, *11–13,* 17, 19–23, *24–25,* 26, *118, 154–155, 160–161;* as music rooms, 32; as office spaces, 36, *37,* 78, *80–81;* with pass-throughs, *52;* with picture galleries, *117;* as play rooms, 33–35; shelves in, *115;* as sitting rooms and guest rooms, 33; as storage rooms, 36; as studios, *158–159*

draperies, 46; for alcoves, *85;* draw, 42; lined, 31, 46; quilted, 46; as room dividers, 14

dressing areas in studio apartments, *146–147*

dressing rooms under lofts, *127*

entertainment centers, 57; in living rooms, 26–30

entertaining in studio apartments, 145–148

entry halls, 134; with picture galleries, *117;* with shelves, *113*

étagères as room dividers, 16, 19

family rooms, in kitchens, 58–62; in living rooms, 18–19, *20–21;* as office spaces, work rooms and guest rooms, *151;* shelves in, *119*

firewood storage under the stairs, *108*

floor painting and stenciling as room dividers, 9

focal points, 19, 112

foyers. *See* entry halls

furniture arrangements, in children's rooms, 68; diagonal, *11;* evaluation of, 3–4; as room dividers, 7, *8,* 10, *11,* 16, 68;

furniture purchase, 136, 139–143

futons, 89, 125

gardening equipment in closets, *101*

Green, Susan Zises, 152, *153*

guest rooms, 87–94; in children's rooms, 65; in dining areas, *153;* in dining rooms and sitting rooms, 33; in kitchens, 60; in living rooms, 30; in sitting rooms and dining rooms, 33

gyms in bedrooms, 44–46

hallways, 136; with picture galleries, *117*

Hart, Robert S., *162–163,* 164

headroom for lofts, 123

hobby closets, 102

home offices, 59, *98;* in kitchens, 61; under lofts, 127; under the stairs, *107*

insulating, of bedrooms, 46, 48; through carpeting, 46–47, 125; through curtains, 46; through wall treatments, 47–48; through window treatments, 46

keeping rooms in dining rooms, *38–39*
Kemper, Scott, 156–157, *158–159*
kitchen equipment under the stairs, *110*
kitchen furniture, 54–62, *57, 58–59,* 60–62, *132*
kitchens, 50–62; as audiovisual centers, 60, 61; with bars, 61; as dens and dining rooms, *54–55, 58–59;* as dining rooms, 51; as family rooms, 58–62; as guest rooms, 60; with home offices, 61; with laundries, 62; under lofts, 127; remodeling of, 50–56; with sewing centers, 62; shelves in *120;* small, 131, *132;* with workshops, 62

ladders. *See* stairs and ladders to lofts
lamps, 49; apothecary, 49; artist's, 49; reading, 33; wall-mounted, 49; *see also* lighting
laundries, in bathrooms, *135;* in closets, *100;* in kitchens, 62
libraries, in dining rooms, 33; and office spaces in living rooms, *22–23;* on lofts, *126*
lighting, in bedrooms, 48–49; fluorescent, 49; incandescent, 49; in kitchens, 51; in living rooms and office spaces, 78; for reading, 42; as room dividers, 9, *17,* 19, 49; for sewing, 42
living rooms, 18–31; *20–21,* 136; as dining rooms, *12–13,* 17, 19, 20–23, *24–25,* 26, 118, *154–155, 160–161;* as dining rooms and conference rooms, *28–29;* as dining rooms and office spaces, *28–29;* as entertainment centers, 26–30; as family rooms, 18–19, *20–21;* as guest rooms, 30; with office spaces, 78; with office spaces and libraries, *22–23;* shelves in, *115*
loft beds. *See* beds
lofts, 123–129; basic *124;* bathrooms under, 127; bridgelike *128;* building permits for, 124; closets under, 127; construction of, 124; dressing rooms under, 127; kitchens under, 127; for libraries, *126;* office spaces under, 127; photographer's darkrooms under, 127; positioning of, 124; sleeping, 125; storage spaces under, 125–128, as studies, *128*
Lone, Robert, 157, *160–161*
loveseats, *28–29,* 33, 40

maid's rooms, 134
music rooms, in dining rooms, 32; on lofts, 125;

office furniture, 77–78
office spaces, 75–86; in bedrooms, *82–85;* behind blinds, *80–81, 84;* in closets, *84–85,* 86, *98;* in dens, *76;* in dining rooms, 36, *37,* 78, *80–81;* behind draperies, *85;* and libraries in living rooms, *22–23;* in living rooms, 78; on lofts, 125; under lofts, 127; behind screens, *85, 86;* in studio apartments, 79, *140–141*
ottomans, 19, 40

painting the floor, 9
panels as room dividers, *6*
pantries, 106; in closets, 102
partitions, 68; permanent, 36, 86
photographer's darkrooms under lofts, 127
pianos, grand, 32; upright 32
picture galleries, in dining rooms, *117,* in entry halls, *117,* in hallways, *117*

pillows, contour, 70; floor, 19, 70, 125; throw, 23; wedge-shaped, 84

plants as room dividers, *17,* 19

platforms, 7–8, 22, *72–73,* 151; multilevel, 17, 66; as room dividers, 7, 9, *34–35;* for sleeping, *142–143;* as storage spaces, 7; in studio apartments, *142–143*

playhouses, under lofts, *67;* under the stairs, 106, *109*

playrooms in dining rooms, 33–35

powder rooms in closets, 102

room dividers, 5–17; blinds as, *80–81;* carpeting as, *11;* chests of drawers as, *10;* in children's rooms, 68–69; draperies as, 14; étàgeres as, 16; floor painting and stenciling as, 9; furniture arrangements as, 7, *8,* 10, *11,* 16, 68; lighting as, 9, *17;* panels as, *6;* plants as, *17,* 19; platforms as, 7, 9, *34–35;* rugs as, 9; screens as, *12–13,* 14, *15,* 86; shelves as, 16, 68, 137; walls as, 14, 16

rooms, L-shaped, 16; small, 150–164; for teenagers, 70, *72–73,* 74

rugs, area, 9, 19; as room dividers, 9

saunas in closets, 102

Schaefer, Paul. *See* Cobuild Associates

screens, for closets, *85;* folding, 14, 46, 68, 93; latticework, *12–13;* paneled, *6, 15,* 34; as room dividers, *12–13,* 14, *15*

seating arrangements under the stairs, *111*

sewing centers, in closets, *84, 99;* in kitchens, 62; under the stairs, 108

shelves, 112–122; for books, 7, 36, 42, 68, 125; as bedside tables, 112; in children's rooms, 119; as china cupboards, 112; as counterspaces, *122;* as desks, 112; in dining areas, *116, 118;* in dining rooms and living rooms, *115;* as dressing tables, 112, *121;* in entry halls, *113;* in family rooms, *119;* in kitchens, 51, *120,*

132; L-shaped, *119;* on lofts, 125; materials for, 114, 117; mounting of, 119–120, 122; as room dividers, 16, *137;* as sideboards, 112; for storage, 112; supports for, *114;* temporary, 70; triangular, *118*

sitting rooms, in bedrooms, 40–42, *41, 44–45;* and guest rooms in dining rooms, 33

skylights, 51

sofas, 7, 87–88; convertible, 30, 88; L-shaped groupings of, 18; platform, *89;* sleep, 58, 85; slip covering of, 19; standard, 58

soundproofing, of bedrooms, 46–48; through carpeting, 46–47; through ceiling treatments, 48; of children's rooms, 65; through curtains, 46; through wall treatments, 47–48; through window treatments, 46

space considerations in studio apartments, 144–145

stairs, under. *See* under the stairs

stairs and ladders to loft, *124, 126, 127, 128*

stenciling the floor, 9

storage space, 40, 69; built-in, 138; inside platforms, 7; on shelves, 112; under the stairs, 105–111

storage rooms in dining rooms, 36

studios, in bedrooms, *162–163; 158–159*

studio apartments, 139–149, *140–141, 146–147*

studies on lofts, *128*

study space, 63

TV. *See* audiovisual center, audiovisual equipment

table tops, 19; protection of, 34

tables, card, 28; cocktail, 19; coffee, 23, 24, 26, 30; conference, 82; dining, 7, 26, 30; dressing, *121;* dressing, in closet, *96;* drop-leaf, *8,* 26, *27,* 42; end, 26; fold-down leaf, built into wall unit, 26; handkerchief, 28; nesting, 26; Parsons, 23, 24; 26, 42, 56, *162–163;*

pedestal, 26; skirted, 26, 40; sofa, 26, 29; tip-top, 26; tray, 26
telephone booths, 108; in closets, 102
toy storage, 19, 34, 65, 70, 106
typewriters, 77, 78
typing tables, 78

under the stairs, beds, 111; firewood, *108;* home offices, *107;* kitchen equipment, *110;* playhouses, 106, *109;* seating arrangements, *111;* storage space, 106–111; wine racks, *107*

walls, half, 16; mirrored, 45; new, partial, 16, 17; proscenium, 16; as room dividers, 14; treatment of, for soundproofing and insulating, 47–48; upkeep of, 31
wall units, *20–21;* for office spaces, 36
washer/dryer set. *See* laundries
weightlifting machines, 46
Weiner, Jean. *See* Cobuild Associates
Weiss, Jeffrey, 152, *154–155*
window treatments as soundproofing and insulating, 46
wine cellars, in closets, 105; under the stairs, *110*
wine racks under the stairs, *110*
workshops, 108; in closets, 105; in kitchens, 62; under lofts, 127